EDITOR: LEE JOHNSON

NEW VANGUARD

LEOPARD 1
MAIN BATTLE TANK
1965-1995

Text by
MICHAEL JERCHEL
Colour plates by
PETER SARSON

First published in Great Britain in 1995 by
Osprey, an imprint of Reed Consumer Books Ltd.
Michelin House, 81 Fulham Road,
London SW3 6RB
and Auckland, Melbourne, Singapore and Toronto

© Copyright 1995 Reed International Books Ltd.

All rights reserved. Apart from any fair dealing for the purpose of private study, research, criticism or review, as permitted under the Copyright Designs and Patents Act, 1988, no part of this publication may be reproduced, stored in a retrieval system, or transmitted in any form or by any means, electronic, electrical, chemical, mechanical, optical, photocopying, recording or otherwise, without the prior permission of the copyright owner. Enquiries should be addressed to the Publishers.

ISBN 1 85532 520 9

Filmset in Great Britain
Printed through World Print Ltd, Hong Kong

Author's Note

The author would like to thank the following individuals and companies for their invaluable advice and assistance during the preparation of this book: Birgit Baumgart of MaK System Gesellschaft mbH, who provided detailed information and additional photographs; Herr Kratz of BWB, for help with Leopard designation systems; and Sabine Rotter, Christopher Foss, Steven Zaloga, Valerio del Grande, Uwe Schnellbacher, Uwe Remmers, Andreas Kirchhoff, Thomas Laber and Waldemar Trojca. Special thanks are due to Herr Zickwolff of Krauss-Maffei for providing some excellent photographs and to Holger Veh for allowing me to photograph the Leopard 1 A1 A2 (2nd batch) which forms part of his splendid collection of armoured vehicles at the Motor-Technica-Museum in Bad Oeynhausen.

Artist's Note

Readers may care to note the original paintings from which the colour plates in this book were prepared are available for private sale. All reproduction copyright whatsoever is retained by the publisher. All enquiries should be addressed to:

Peter Sarson
Room C1, Ellerslie Chambers
Minton Road
Bournemouth
Dorset BH1 2EE

The publishers regret that they can enter into no correspondence upon this matter.

Editor's note

Readers may wish to read this title in conjunction with the following Osprey titles:

Elite 10 *Warsaw Pact Ground Forces*
Elite 16 *NATO Armies Today*
New Vanguard 2 *M1 Abrams Main Battle Tank*
New Vanguard 3 *T-72 Main Battle Tank*

If you would like to receive more information about Osprey Military books, The Osprey Messenger is a regular news letter which contains articles, new title information and special offers. To join free of charge please write to:

**Osprey Military Messenger,
PO Box 5, Rushden,
Northants, NN10 6YX**

LEOPARD I MAIN BATTLE TANK

DESIGN AND DEVELOPMENT

Development of the Leopard 1 can be traced back to November 1956, when the operational requirement for a new battle tank was formulated by the Federal German Armed Forces (Bundeswehr). The first tanks operated by the Bundeswehr were the US-built M47 and M48, which were cheap and available in quantity. But it was recognised that the M47 in particular was very much an interim design – a view evidently shared by the US Army, as some 8,500 of the 9,100 M47s produced were exported. With the M47 virtually obsolete, what the Bundeswehr badly needed was a thoroughly modern main battle tank (MBT), with the armour protection and main gun performance to take on the vastly superior numbers of excellent MBTs (as well as other armoured vehicles) operated by the Red Army.

In 1957, the Bundeswehr's requirement for a '30 ton MBT' specified a power-to-weight ratio of 30 PS/tonne; an air-cooled multi-fuel engine; a range of 350 km; either torsion bar or hydropneumatic suspension; an overall width not exceeding 3150 mm; and sufficient armour to withstand hits from 20 mm rounds at close range. The main gun should be capable of penetrating 150 mm of sloped armour, while the ammunition load should at least be equal to that of current US tanks.

Franco-German Project

In June 1957 Germany and France signed a co-operation agreement to develop a common tank, designated 'Standard-Panzer'. Two German and one French design team would be responsible for the construction of four German and two French prototypes of the vehicle. In September 1958 Italy joined the development programme. Work started in 1958, Germany's 'Team A' (Firmengruppe A) consisting of Porsche, MaK, Luther & Jung (under leadership of Porsche KG). Similarly, 'Team B' (Firmengruppe B) was made up by

The prototype A II, seen here during an exhibition in Bonn, had a ranging MG on the gun mantlet and lacked the optical rangefinding system. Also of note are the protective screens around the headlights and the early style exhaust grills. (Archiv Laber)

One of the 50 pre-series vehicles seen during trials at Munster. The 'O series' re-introduced the optical rangefinder, but still had only a rectangular hatch at the loader's station and used the old rhomb style of tactical marking on the glacis. The tactical marking assumed the familiar rectangular style on introduction of the series vehicle (1st batch). (Archiv Laber)

Ruhrstahl, Rheinstahl-HANOMAG and Henschel (under leadership of Warneke office of Ruhrstahl); Wegmann and Rheinmetall were awarded the contract to develop a common turret.

The first wooden mock-ups were completed in 1959, followed in January 1961 by the first two of the planned four prototypes. Both of these 'A 1s' were built by Team A (one by Jung/Jungenthal, the other supplied by MaK/Kiel), and were each fitted with a Mercedes-Benz MB 837 A eight-cylinder engine. Both vehicles weighed 35 tonnes.

The tank was originally fitted with a 90 mm main gun, but this was replaced by a 105 mm L7 gun during 1961 for trials purposes. Rheinmetall had tried to develop its own 105 mm gun from the outset, firing a new French hollow charge round, but as the excellent British-designed 105 mm L7 was already available with a wide range of existing tank ammunition, this programme was dropped for sound logistical and cost reasons. The L7 was capable of firing HEAT (High Explosive Anti-Tank); APDS (Armour Piercing Discarding Sabot); and HESH/HEP (High Explosive Squash Head/High Explosive Anti-Personnel). Accordingly, in autumn 1962 a total of 1,500 L7A1 guns were purchased for the new tank. The upper rear end of the gun breech had to be sloped so as to meet the requirement for a maximum main gun depression of -9° within the Leopard turret. Thus modified, the weapon was designated L7A3.

The two 'B I' prototypes designed and built by Team B were not ready until September 1961. The delay was caused by problems encountered during the development of such advanced features as the new HANOMAG two-cycle multi-fuel engine, the hydrostatic steering system and the hydro-pneumatic springing/shock absorption for its running gear and road wheels (six per side). The hydro-pneumatic system allowed the vehicle to be lowered or raised by altering the volume of oil in the cylinders. Comparative trials with the 'A I' and 'B I' prototypes were completed in April 1962, the 'A I' being selected for further development.

Although Team B received an order for six prototypes 'B IIs', it was clear that the complexity of the vehicle would severely delay its entry into service. When Team A received an order for 27 prototype 'A IIs', Team B had no option but stop development of the 'B II' for financial reasons.

The Early Prototype

Building of the first prototype 'A II', internally known as 'Porschetyp 773', had already started in September 1960 in anticipation of the official order, and improvements suggested by trials with the 'A I' were incorporated in the new vehicle.

In its original form the Leopard 1 (1st batch) entered service with the Bundeswehr in 1965. The apertures for the co-axial MG and TZF gunner's scope have been sealed with stoppers. A 7.62 mm Rheinmetall MG 1 (derived from the MG 42 of WW2) is mounted on the revised loader's hatch fitted to series production vehicles. Note the protective fabric attached to the muzzle of the main gun. (Krauss-Maffei)

In its original form the Leopard 1 (4th batch) entered service in 1968, and is distinguished by its revised exhaust grills. This vehicle also mounts the XSW-30-U infra-red/white-light searchlight on the gun mantlet. The searchlight is normally carried in the stowage bin at the turret rear when not in use. (Krauss-Maffei Via Archiv Laber)

Armour protection was increased to 70 mm thickness, vehicle width was also increased by 70 mm, and a new Mercedes-Benz MB 838 ten-cylinder multi-fuel engine, developing 830 PS, was installed. The chassis and interior of the vehicle was slightly revised and total weight increased to 36.2 tonnes.

Wegmann and Rheinmetall manufactured 32 turrets for the prototype 'A IIs', which differed slightly in shape from those made for the 'A I'; the centre of gravity and the fume extraction system were also changed. 'A II' turrets were equipped with the 105 mm L7A3 main gun and a 12.7 mm ranging machine gun (MG), which was installed to the left of the main gun above the co-axial MG, in lieu of the coincidence rangefinder.

In autumn 1962 the 'A II' was evaluated by Panzer-Lehrbataillon (training battalion) 93 (abbreviated PzBtl. L93), attached to Kampftruppenschule 2, the German armour school in Munster. The effectiveness of the ranging MG was considered to be markedly inferior in

Soon after delivery, the first four batches of the Leopard 1 were modernised to A1 standard. Between 1975-77 these vehicles were further upgraded as Leopard 1A1A1 with add-on turret armour and other changes. This vehicle is from the original 1st batch, recognisable by its square intercom box on the right-hand side of the rear plate. The stowage box to the left contains tools. (Michael Jerchel)

comparison with the coincidence rangefinder, the latter's reinstatement being demanded for series production vehicles.

The French meanwhile were busy at Atelier de Construction d'Issy-les-Moulineaux, the first AMX-30 prototype for comparative trials being ready in 1962. While testing continued with the prototype 'A II', the German defence committee decided to purchase a pre-series batch of 50 tanks, also known as the 'O-series'. These tanks were built by MaK (16 vehicles), Luther & Jordan (17) and Jung-Jungenthal (17), with the first tank becoming available for testing in June 1963. 'O-series' tanks were duly equipped with the coincidence rangefinder in 'Series III' turrets, but otherwise differed only slightly from the prototype 'A II'. The combat weight increased to 39.6 tonnes. Field and acceptance testing (which preceded unit evaluation) was conducted in June 1963 when 13 of the pre-series tanks were served with Wehrtechnische Dienststelle (WTD) 91 at Meppen – seven for gunnery and six for locomotive/driving trials.

Between August-October 1963 comparative trials were conducted between the German and French designed prototypes at Mailly de Camp, Bourges and Satory (France), and continued in Meppen (Germany) – interestingly, all under Italian supervision. The trials demonstrated that the German tank had the edge over the French AMX-30. But intriguingly a change in defence

The first two batches of the Leopard 1 were delivered without hookeyes, but as an interim measure they were added to the vehicle's rear, as revealed by this Leopard 1A1A1 having its turret removed by a Bergepanzer 2. (Michael Jerchel)

Camouflaged with bands of mud, this Leopard 1A1A1 (1st batch) of Panzerbataillon 354 takes part in Exercise 'Counter Strike' at the Bonnland village of KTS 1, the German infantry school in Hammelburg. The vehicle is equipped with a Hoffmann-Werke gunfire simulation device on the main gun and has the later (longer) towing cables attached.

policy, together with funding problems, suddenly prevented the French from purchasing any new tanks before 1965. Not surprisingly, this turn of events ended Franco-German efforts to produce a common or 'Standard' MBT and both countries went on to pursue their own, national, tank development programmes. The first AMX-30s were delivered to the French Army in the autumn of 1966 by which time she had withdrawn from NATO, only one year after Germany commenced series production of the Leopard. Italy decided to be different and purchased the American M60A1 instead.

On 1 October 1963 the 'Standard' tank was officially named 'Leopard', an appropriate choice considering Germany's wartime pedigree with the formidable Tiger and Panther. Unit trials of the pre-series tanks were carried out between July 1964 and October 1965 by PzBtl. L93 in Munster. At the beginning of these trials a Leopard demonstrated its fording capability by crossing the river Rhine near Cologne to a depth of 4.20 m using a special snorkel device. The trials vindicated the design of the new tank and relatively few modifications were required (170 to be exact) before the Leopard was cleared for series production. On 22 August 1963, an order for 1,500 Leopards was placed after the German parliament (Bundestag) approved funding for the fiscal year 1964. The first series production Leopard (later re-designated Leopard 1 to differentiate it from the Leopard 2), left the newly built assembly line of prime contractor Krauss-Maffei AG in Munich on 9 September 1965. The Leopard 1 was built in six batches (or 'Lots'), a small number also being built by Krupp MaK in Kiel.

SERIES PRODUCTION

The 1st batch

The 500 tanks in the first production batch (Fahrgestell Nr. 5001-5999) were built between September 1965-July 1966, replacing the M47 within the divisions of 1st (GE) Corps. The Leopard 1 has an all-welded hull. The running gear consists of seven road wheels per side, with four return rollers and idler wheel at the front and drive sprocket at the rear. Torsion bar suspension is employed, with the 1st, 2nd, 3rd, 6th and 7th road wheel stations having additional hydraulic shock absorbers. The Diehl D139E2 double pin

Bearing the name **Gneisenau** *on the first section of add-on turret armour, this plain olive green (RAL 6014) Leopard 1A1A1 takes a break after an exercise at Bergen-Hohne in 1989. This vehicle came from the third batch, as denoted by the two hookeyes and exhaust grills. It also displays a variation in the stowage of tow cables, which are crossed behind the turret from one side to the other. The protective base plate of the gunfire simulator is stored in the rear basket, partly obscuring the turret number '366'. (Michael Jerchel)*

tracks, with rubber-bushed end connectors, have vulcanised rubber sections on the track links; there are 84 links per track.

The driver's position is situated to the right front of the hull. Protection is provided by a lift-and-swing type hatch that opens to the left. For driving under armoured cover, the driver has three vision periscopes available, the centre block being interchangeable with an (active) IR-sight for night operations. The cast turret is mounted in the centre of the hull and is manned by the commander and the gunner (seated below and in front of the commander) in the right half, with the loader in the left half. The loader has a single-piece hatch cover, opening to the rear. A 7.62 mm MG 1 (later replaced by a MG 3) for air defence is mounted to the ring mount, operated by the loader, who has two observation periscopes available when under armour.

A total of 60 rounds are carried for the 105 mm L7A3 rifled gun. Most of the ammunition (42 rounds) is stored in a special magazine in the hull to the left of the driver; three rounds are held in a ready use triple rack in front of it, and a further 15 are racked in the turret. Various types of British, American and German ammunition can be fired, including APDS, HEAT, HESH/HEP as well as smoke, canister and target illumination rounds. The normal ammunition mix is 31 APDS, 26 HESH/HEP and three smoke rounds.

The gunner's primary sight is the Turmentfernungsmesser (TEM) 1A rangefinder sight (with 1720 mm basis length), which can be selectively used in either stereoscopic or coincidence mode. It is linked to the unstabilised 105 mm L7A3 main gun and has a selective magnification of x8 or x16. The external optical heads of the TEM-1A are situated to the left and right side of the turret in armoured housings. A small protective flap in front of each housing is opened by the gunner from inside the turret prior to operation. The gunner also has the TZF 1A telescope with a magnification of x8 available, mounted to the right side of and co-axially with the main gun. The co-axial 7.62 mm MG 1 with 1,250 rounds mounted to the left side of the main gun was subsequently replaced by the MG 3.

For the commander a swivel-mounted independent sight is provided, the Turmrundblick-Pankrat

(TRP) 1A, a zoom-periscope with a magnification of x6 up to x20, which is installed in the turret roof immediately in front of the commander's station. When the TRP periscope is automatically slaved to the main gun, the commander has the option of overriding the gunner if required. A further eight periscopes give the commander an excellent all-round view; one of these can be replaced by an (active) IR-sight for night operations.

Four 76 mm smoke mortars are mounted to each side of the turret and are fired electrically

Digital SEM 80/90 radios were first issued to the Bundeswehr in 1985, their subsequent fitment to the Leopard 1 being identified by the vehicle's shorter antennae and new designators. This Leopard 1A1A3 is taking part in the REFORGER 88 FTX 'Certain Challenge' in September 1988. (Michael Jerchel)

either as single rounds or in salvo. A full reload of eight smoke rounds is carried inside the tank. The mounting for the XSW-30-U searchlight is located on the left of the mantlet above the main gun. Operated in either IR or whitelight modes, the searchlight has a maximum range of 1200 and

This is the Leopard 1A1A4, equipped with the PZB 200 low-light-level TV camera system (visible on the gun mantlet next to the searchlight) and SEM 80/90 radios. On exercise at Bergen-Hohne, this vehicle is serving with Panzeraufklärungsbataillon 12, the armoured reconnaissance battalion of 12th (GE) Panzer Division. As required by German traffic regulations, the orange RKL warning ('Whoopie') light is mounted when driving on public roads. (Volkmar Rösner)

The A1 and A2 are difficult to tell apart, but this is known to be a company of Leopard 1A2 of Panzerlehrbataillon 93 at Munster. As may be seen, these A2s have yet to receive thermal sleeves for their main guns. (MaK System)

This depot view of a Leopard 1A2A1 shows the camouflage pattern introduced in 1985. The Leopard 1A2A1 has oval outer panels over the optical sight heads, unlike the circular covers fitted to the first to fourth batches. The power socket for the searchlight is located between the optical head and the national emblem. (Thomas Laber)

1500 m respectively. When not in use, the searchlight is stored in a stowage bin at the turret rear. (Alternatively, the slightly modified XSW-30-V searchlight is available on later versions of the Leopard.) Two SEM 25 and one SEM 35 radios are installed in the turret behind and to the right of the commander's station. Both radio sets operate in the 26-70 MHz band, maximum range being 25 and 12 km respectively. The radio antennae are mounted to the left and right on the turret behind the crew stations.

The engine compartment is at the rear, separated from the fighting compartment by a fire-proof bulkhead. The MB 838 CaM-500 liquid-cooled 37.4 litre ten-cylinder V-90 four-stroke multi-fuel engine develops 610 kW (830 PS). The engine is normally run on diesel fuel (NATO designation F-54), consuming about 190 litres per 100 km. The two fuel tanks located inside the engine compartment to the left and right hand side have a total capacity of 1010 litres (reduced to 985 litres on later Leopards). Internal exhaust outlets for the engine are situated on either side of the hull at the rear. Quick disconnect couplings allow the entire powerpack (engine, cooling system and transmission) to be exchanged in the field within 20 minutes. The sealed cooling system for the power pack is designed to operate in temperatures between -40 to +40°C, pre-heating prior to engine start being necessary below -18°C. The engine is started using a 15 PS/19 kW generator, together with eight 12-volt batteries. The ZF4 HP250 combined steer-and-shift transmission is epicyclic and coupled directly to the engine. Four forward and two reverse gears are available through a torque converter and lock-up clutch, enabling the tank to turn on-the-spot if required. The transmission automatically changes

This Leopard 1A2A1 of PzBtl. 184 is fitted with a snorkel (mounted on the commander's cupola) for deep fording up to a depth of 4 m. (Michael Jerchel)

gear within the range pre-selected by the driver. The gears are shifted electro-hydraulically, without loss of tractive effort.

Four, 5.5 kg Halon fire-extinguisher bottles are installed behind the driver's seat on the right-hand side. The bottles are connected to hoses and pipes and are activated automatically by the electronic fire detection system, or manually via the control panel in the driver's compartment. The ventilation system is completely self-contained and incorporates an overpressure NBC capability.

The Leopard 1 is able to ford water obstacles 1.20 m deep (wading) without any special preparations or loss of combat effectiveness. But before fording at a depth of 2.25 m (deep-wading), about ten minutes' special preparation is needed to seal the tank. This process includes fitting a foldable snorkel, stored above the magazine to the left of the driver, to the commander's cupola. Two bilge pumps remove any water entering the tank.

Combat weight of the Leopard 1 is 40.0 tonnes, the empty weight being 38.0 tonnes. Its maximum forward speed on roads is 65 km/h, but this is limited to 50 km/h in Bundeswehr service. In second reverse gear the maximum speed achievable is 25 km/h.

The 2nd, 3rd and 4th Batches

Built July 1966-July 1967; Fahrgestell Nr. 6001-6999. A total of 600 vehicles were delivered to the divisions of the Ist and IIIrd (GE) Corps. The 2nd batch differed only in detail. A small gutter was attached at the bottom of the turret rear. The external head-set connectors to the crew's intercom system were now installed in a circular container (instead of a square one) on the rear plate. Deflectors were mounted on the hull to protect the turret ring.

The 3rd batch was built July 1967-August 1968; Fahrgestell Nr. 7001-7999. Altogether 500 tanks were delivered to the divisions of Ist and IIIrd (GE) Corps. The 3rd batch introduced hookeyes above the rear lights and on the vehicle sides at a position above the first road wheel.

The 4th batch was produced between August 1968-February 1970. As this was also an export variant, the Werke Nr. are as follows: 8001-8999

Leopard 1A3 with the protective screens for the TEM 1A stereoscopic/coincidence sights – integrated into the new welded turret – slid open. Camouflage is enhanced with bands and splotches of mud. (MaK System)

Only a few Leopard 1A3 received the new Bundeswehr camouflage scheme, seen here on a vehicle of PzBtl. 304. The yellow patch on the side of the turret is the primer paint background for the battalion badge. (Thomas Laber)

(Bundeswehr); 12001-12999 and 13001-13999 (export). The 4th batch introduced revised exhaust grills with horizontal struts only (preceding batches also had vertical struts). Hookeyes were also fitted.

FIRST MODERNISATION

Leopard 1A1

After delivery of the last tank in the 4th batch, a modernisation programme was launched in 1970 to enhance the combat effectiveness of the Bunderswehr's existing fleet. Most importantly, all Leopards received the Cadillac-Gage main gun stabilisation system. This featured power-elevation from -9 to +20° and full stabilisation in both elevation and traverse (360°). Targets could now be acquired and engaged on the move, and the system significantly increased the probability of a first round hit in a tank duel. The barrel of the 105 mm L7A3 main gun was equipped with a thermal sleeve. Metal-rubber side skirts were added to increase protection against HEAT shaped charges. The older Diehl D139E2 double-pin tracks with vulcanised treads were replaced with the new D640A double-pin tracks with detachable rubber pads. For winter operations, a number of these rubber pads can be replaced by special 'X'-patterned metal pads (grousers) so as to achieve better traction on frozen ground. Understandably, the use of metal pads on public roads is not permitted in peacetime; 20 grousers are stored on the upper glacis plate when not in use. A new snorkel increased the maximum fording depth to 4 m (underwater drive). As before, the snorkel was mounted on top of the commander's station and supplied air to the engine and crew; all openings were sealed or closed by special plugs. Attached to chains mounted on the hull, the plugs are pulled out by simply turning the turret. The IR (active) night sights for the driver and commander were replaced by passive image intensification night sights (Bildverstärkergeräte, BIV). This series of upgrades increased combat weight to 41.5 tonnes and the tank received the new designation Leopard 1A1.

Cast steel turret (5th batch)

Built 1972-1974, the 5th batch included 232 tanks with a cast steel turret of thicker armour. Designated Leopard 1A2, this tank is quite difficult to distinguish from the modernised Leopard

Leopard 1A3 of PzBtl. 304 with snorkel for deep fording (underwater drive). The snorkel is supplied as required in three parts and is not normally stored inside the tank. The badge on the mantlet depicts a fox with a shield bearing the Roman numeral III; the battalion badge is applied on the side of the turret. (Thomas Laber)

Short foldable snorkel at the ready, a Leopard 1A3A1 of 2nd Company/PzBtl. 304 enters a training pool so as to simulate fording operations. The snorkel ensures a supply of air to the engine and crew in up to 2.25 m of water and is stored inside the tank when not required. A 'Hoffman device' gunfire simulator is fitted to the gun barrel. (Michael Jerchel)

1A1 vehicles of the 4th batch, the former having oval (instead of circular) cover plates on the heads of its optical rangefinders. The Leopard 1A2 never received add on turret armour, but it did get an improved NBC protection system. Most vehicles from this batch saw service with the 6th (GE) Panzer grenadier Division, which trained extensively with the Danish Army.

Welded turret (5th batch)

The remaining 110 vehicles from this batch were fitted with a new welded turret incorporating spaced armour and a wedge-shaped gun mantlet. Although the degree of armour protection

Leopard 1A4 of PzBtl. 282 displaying early style markings on the glacis plate and variations of the mud camouflage. The armoured screens for the EMES 12 A1 stereoscopic rangefinder are in the open position and the optical head of the PERI R 12 may be seen between the gunfire simulator on the barrel and searchlight. (MaK System)

remained unchanged, the internal volume of the turret was increased by 1.5 m2. The improved TRP 2A independent sight was installed for the commander. This version received the designation Leopard 1A3 and the majority went to the 10th and 12th Panzer Divisions. Fahrgestell Nr. for the Leopard 1A2/A3 are 14001-14999. The combat weight of both vehicles was 42.4 tonnes.

The 6th batch

The Bundeswehr took delivery of the first 250 vehicles from this batch in 1974, designated Leopard 1A4. This version had the welded turret introduced with the Leopard 1A3, but with a new integrated fire control system. This comprised the PERI R12 stabilised independent sight for the commander, and the EMES 12A1 stereoscopic rangefinder and gunner's primary sight coupled to the fully stabilised main gun, controlled by a ballistic computer. The optical head of the PERI R12 is installed immediately in front of the commander's cupola on the turret roof. Installation of the fire control system used up additional space and consequently the ammunition load was reduced to 55 rounds, of which 42 were stored in the magazine to the left of the driver and 13 in ready use racks in the turret. This batch saw service with 10th Panzer Division of IInd (GE) Corps, with a few vehicles going to the German armour school.

SECOND MODERNISATION

Leopard 1A1A1

From 1975 to 1977 all vehicles in the 1st to 4th batches, known as the Leopard 1A1, were retrofitted with additional turret armour developed by Blohm und Voss. The armour consists of steel plates with a two-faced rubber lining, being attached to the turret (including the turret basket at the rear) with shock-proof spacers and nuts. The gun mantlet received a wedge shaped, add-on armour made of steel plates. If an engine change is required, the first plate of this sectional add-on armour must be removed so as to ensure adequate clearance. Finally, the combustion air intake filters were considerably improved. Following modification, the vehicle was re-designated Leopard 1A1 A1. The add-on armour increased combat weight to 42.4 tonnes.

Improved night vision

In 1980, the Panzer-Ziel und Beobachtungsgerät (PZB 200) entered service with the Bundeswehr. Produced by Telefunken, the PZB 200 is a passive image intensification night vision system for aiming and observation. It consists mainly of the low-

A small hatch for the loader is retained on the cast turret versions (in this case a Leopard 1A5) despite the add-on armour, a section of which opens and closes so as to allow the crew to eject of spent ammunition casings. (Michael Jerchel)

light-level television (LLLTV) camera, mounted on the gun mantlet in a protective bar-shaped housing to the right-hand side of the vehicle's centreline. The PZB 200 system intensifies the night scene and transfers the image to TV monitor viewed by the gunner and/or commander. A control panel is used to focus the lenses and to open or close the diaphragm. Initially only a few Leopard 1 were equipped with the PZB 200, which was intended as an interim fit for the Leopard 2 in lieu of its planned thermal night vision system. When the Leopard 2 was fitted with thermal sights, their PZB 200s were transferred to Leopard 1 fleet from the 1st to 4th batches (re-designated Leopard 1A1A2) as well as the cast steel turret 5th batch (re-designated Leopard 1A2A1) and welded turret 5th batch (re-designated Leopard 1A3A1). The 6th batch (Leopard 1A4) was not fitted with the PZB 200 system.

Leopard 1A5

In 1980 a research programme was undertaken to study further improvements to the Leopard 1, the aim being to maintain its survivability and combat effectiveness beyond the year 2000. The tank was originally designed to combat the hordes of Soviet T-55s and T-62s, but now faced the more modern (and formidable) T-64B, T-72B, and T-72M1. The expected T-80B posed an even greater threat; the Leopard 1 would now have to operate effectively at night and in poor visibility as well as shoot quickly and accurately on the move. Accordingly, a new thermal sight and fire control/ballistic computer was specified. In addition, better ammunition for the 105 mm main gun would be needed so as to ensure good penetration performance against increasingly sophisticated Soviet armour.

UPGRADING THE LEOPARD I

After comparative trials, in December 1983 the Krupp-Atlas Electronik (KAE) EMES 18 fire control system was selected in preference to the AEG-Telefunken EMES 17, and Carl Zeiss EMES 12A4. With Wegmann as prime contractor, it was planned to convert some 1,225 Leopard 1A1A1 (1st to 4th batches). In the event, one vehicle was destroyed by fire, reducing the eventual total to 1,224. Re-designated Leopard 1A5, the first modified vehicle was delivered to the Bundeswehr in early 1987.

The EMES 18 fire control system was developed from the proven EMES 15 installed in the Leopard 2 and shares many common components. At its heart is the Hauptzielfernrohr (HZF) or primary sight, the optical block of which is installed in an armoured housing on top of the turret to the right-hand side. This housing con-

A Leopard 1A5 (former 1st batch) demonstrates its gun stabilisation system, which enables the tank to fire on move with a high degree of first-round hit probability. (Michael Jerchel)

tains the thermal imaging system (made by Carl Zeiss) for target observation and acquisition at night or in bad weather, as well as the laser rangefinder. Two flaps provide protection when the sight or rangefinder is not in use. The TEM 2A stereoscopic sight was removed, the resultant apertures on the turret sides being sealed with circular armoured plates.

The ballistic computer is installed below the commander's seat on the bottom base plate of the turret. Derived from the one used in Leopard 2 (which has a 120 mm main gun), the computer was modified to be compatible with the parameters of the 105 mm L7A3 gun. The system stores ballistic information for up to seven different types of ammunition and is able to compute targeting solutions out to 4000 m. A vertical sensor automatically eliminates any cant angle errors (which can occur when the vehicle is traversing a slope) from the ballistic computations. A built-in test/fault system locates any malfunctioning components.

The computer control panel, installed above the gunner's seat, is common to Leopard 2. The commander's TRP independent sight, was retained but is slightly taller for a clear view over the housing of the EMES 18. The original telescope (Turmzielfernrohr, TZF 1A) for the gunner remained unchanged. A muzzle reference system was introduced, a Carl Zeiss collimator being fitted at the end of the barrel for the gunner to rapidly check the adjustment of the HZF primary sight and main gun. The new SRK (Steuer und Regelkonzept) servo-hydraulic turret control system became available during the Leopard 1A5 conversion programme. From 1988, those vehicles already converted and delivered with the existing Cadillac-Gage system were retrofitted with the SRK.

A crucial part of the Leopard 1 upgrade was the introduction of more effective main gun ammunition, specifically APFSDS (Armour Piercing Discarding Sabot) rounds with advanced armour penetration material. This new ammunition was designated DM23 and DM33. Interestingly, a single Leopard 1A5 was fitted with a Rheinmetall 120 mm smooth-bore gun for trials purposes. Although successful (all Leopard 1A5 being adapted to carry the weapon), plans to retrofit the 120 mm gun were eventually abandoned as being too impractical.

The running gear was also further improved with the addition of strengthened torsion bar suspension and shock absorber mountings. Other

A Leopard 1A5 of 2nd Company/PzBtl. 14 during a live firing exercise on range 11 at Bergen, Norway. This is a former 1st batch vehicle, as denoted by the square intercom box to the right of the rear plate. (Michael Jerchel)

Another Leopard 1A5 of 2nd Company/PzBtl. 14, but this time identified as a former 4th batch vehicle by the revised exhaust grill. Mixing different Leopard batches was not unusual, even at platoon level. A cable reel for communication purposes is attached to the turret rear; the angular fittings are for stowing camouflage netting. (Michael Jerchel)

detail changes included fitting hookeyes to vehicles in the 1st and 2nd batches and adding a cleaning system (subsequently installed on most Leopard 1) for the driver's vision blocks.

New generation radios

In the late 1980s, digital SEM 80/90 VHF radios were issued to the Bundeswehr. Much smaller and lighter than the preceding generation, the SEM 80/90 is a modular design: connecting a 40 watt amplifier to the basic SEM 80 produces the SEM 90. Following the installation of these radios a new series of vehicle designators were issued to the various batches:

New Designators

Leopard 1A1A1 (SEM 80/90)	Leopard 1A1A3
Leopard 1A1A2 (SEM 80/90, PZB 200)	Leopard 1A1A4
Leopard 1A2 (SEM 80/90)	Leopard 1A2A2
Leopard 1A2A1 (SEM 80/90, PZB 200)	Leopard 1A2A3
Leopard 1A3 (SEM 80/90)	Leopard 1A3A2
Leopard 1 A3A1 (SEM 80/90, PZB 200)	Leopard 1A3A3
Leopard 1 A5 (SEM 80/90)	Leopard 1A5A1

A new designator was prepared for the Leopard 1A4, but it was phased out before receiving the PZB 200 LLLTV camera or SEM 80/90 radios.

17

A Leopard 1A5A1 (former 4th batch) negotiates an obstacle. The Leopard can climb over vertical obstacles up to 1.15 m high and cross trenches up to 2.5 m wide. (Michael Jerchel)

INSIDE THE LEOPARD 1A5

Engaging a target

To steer the tank, the driver simply turns the control lever left or right according to the direction of travel; steering is regenerative. The gearbox allows selection of either 'V' (forward); 'N' (neutral); 'R' (reverse) or 'W' (turn). Four forward gears are available: maximum speed in first gear is 13 km/h; in second 24 km/h; in third 37 km/h (includes shifting of second gear); and in fourth (includes shifting of second and third gears) 62 km/h. In 'kick down' mode, the Leopard 1 takes 12 seconds to accelerate from 0-100 m. Two reverse gears are available, maximum speed being 24 km/h. To turn on the spot, the tank is first halted, 'W' selected on the gearbox and the control lever moved in the direction of rotation.

In combat, the loader takes one of the 13 ready use rounds (either a DM33 APFSDS-T or a DM12 HEAT-MP-T), and loads the gun. The total combat load consists of 55 rounds (a further 42 are stored in the magazine to the left of the driver). The breech of the 105 mm L7A3 main gun is semi-automatic, opening after each round is fired. Empty shell cases are ejected into an attached bag. The breech area is fenced in to protect the crew.

When the commander has identified a target, the gunner takes over to engage it as soon as the commander has slewed around the turret to the target's azimuth. The gunner identifies the target through his HZF sighting channel of the EMES 18 and conducts the laser rangefinding tasks.

Powder temperature, cant angle automatic correction value, atmospheric conditions, vehicle altitude and target speed, are fed into the fire control

After German unification in October 1990, the Bundeswehr phased out the T-55 and T-72 MBTs and replaced them with the Leopard 1A5 among the new Panzerbatallions in Eastern Germany. This Leopard 1A5 was issued to PzBtl. 403 in Schwerin, where it poses with a BRDM-2/SPW 40P2, remnant of the disbanded Motor Rifle Regiment 27/8th Motor Rifle Division. (Michael Jerchel)

computer, which continuously calculates elevation and lead angles for the main gun. Command signals are transmitted to the armament control system, which re-lays the main gun without disturbing the line-of-sight, and finally the off-set gun aiming mark is generated for the optic sighting channel. When the gunner has the aiming mark coincident with the actual gun position, the firing circuit is complete and the main gun may be fired.

About 30 years after the introduction of the Leopard 1, the Bundeswehr's order of battle still includes 730 Leopard 1A5 and A5A1 MBTs, all now exclusively employed by panzer grenadier brigades following the recent reorganisation (Heeresstruktur 5) of the German army.

A Leopard 1 driver training tank travelling across country. The turret is replaced by an observation cabin with dual controls, a dummy gun barrel ensuring that the trainee driver is fully aware of the vehicle's overall dimensions. (Sabine Rotter)

THE LEOPARD I IN FOREIGN SERVICE

European Allies

The Belgian version is based on the German 4th batch (a few vehicles being from the 3rd batch), and is designated Leopard 1 BE. Belgium was the first foreign country to place an order (in 1967), and deliveries started in 1968.

The Leopard 1 BE in its original form closely resembled German 4th batch vehicles, but had the 7.62 mm FN MAG. As from 1975, the vehicles were equipped with extra stowage boxes to the hull sides, a Cadillac-Gage gun stabilisation system and the main gun received a thermal sleeve. In addition, initial vehicles from the third batch equipped with the gun stabilisation system were fitted with a SABCA fire control system. This consists of an optical sight with an integral laser rangefinder, analogue computer and crosswind velocity sensor. The computer calculates the angles between the main gun axis and the line-of-sight from the range of the target and other fire control relevant data measured by the sensors, such as powder temperature, cant and rate of turret traverse, cross wind, external temperature, and gun wear. After this data is computed (in a fraction of a second), the cross-hair in the gunner's sight is displaced in azimuth and elevation. The gunner now only has to bring back the cross-hair onto the target. (The SABCA fire control system has been adopted by Australia and Canada for their Leopards.) From early 1980, the two other remaining batches were retrofitted with the SABCA FCS.

In 1988 one vehicle was fitted with the add-on armour developed by Blohm und Voss, a new fire control computer, and a thermal day/night sight developed by SABCA and OIP with an integrated laser rangefinder. The latter was installed in a similar armoured housing to the German Leopard 1A5. Deliveries of the modernised Leopard 1 BE are expected to begin in 1997 at a rate of four vehicles per month. Belgium took delivery of 334 Leopard 1 BE MBTs, 12 driver training tanks, 36 Leopard ARVs, six Armoured Engineer Vehicles and 55 Gepard air defence systems. Planned cuts in military spending will see the number of MBTs reduced to 132 Leopard 1 BE (modernised), the remainder to be sold within three years. The Gepard will be phased out completely.

Denmark ordered 120 Leopard 1 DK in 1974, which were delivered between March 1976 and November 1978. The Danish version is based on the Leopard 1A3 but has extra stowage boxes fit-

Leopard 1 BE of the 4th BN Lanciers at speed on the ring road near range 9, Bergen, in 1993. Between the two stowage boxes at the side of the hull is the exhaust for the diesel driven heating system – most welcome in winter! (Michael Jerchel)

ted to the hull sides. A special camouflage mat, made of rough material, was developed and fixed to the tank's hull, side skirts and turret. Unfortunately, decontamination of this camouflage proved extremely difficult, and the mats were subsequently removed. More recently a modernisation programme was started to retrofit the Danish version with the EMES 18 FCS, leading to the Leopard 1A5 DK. All Danish Leopards may be fitted with a dozer-blade or a TWMP mine clearing device, including the additional 110 Leopard 1A3 ordered from German stocks and also modernised to A5 DK standard, bringing the total to 230 Leopard 1A5 DK.

In 1981 Greece placed an order for 106 Leopard 1 GR MBTs and four ARVs, of which 73 MBTs were built by Krauss-Maffei and the remainder by MaK System in Kiel. The Greek MBTs are based on the Leopard 1A3, but are fitted out with the EMES 12 A3 computerised fire control system and the PZB 200 image intensification system, and were delivered between 1983 and 1984. The Leopard 1 GR's were built by Krauss-Maffei, and received a factory applied camouflage consisting of brown, green, beige and black. Until early 1994, a batch of 75 Leopard 1A5 were delivered by Krauss-Maffei, and the Netherlands delivered 172 Leopard 1 V free of charge under the 'Armament aid' programme.

Although one of the three original countries involved in the development of Leopard 1, Italy did not place its first order until 1970. The first batch of 200 vehicles were delivered by Krauss-Maffei in 1971-1972, a further 400 being built under licence by OTO Melara from 1974. The last Leopard 1 from the original batch was delivered in 1978. Deliveries of an additional 120 vehicles were then completed in 1983. MaK supplied 69 Armoured Recovery Vehicles (ARVs) and 12

Rear quarter view of a Belgian Leopard 1 BE taken at Bergen in 1989, displaying its external similarity to German 4th batch vehicles. Ammunition boxes have been added to the turret basket for extra stowage space. (Michael Jerchel)

Armoured Combat Engineer Vehicles (ACEVs), while OTO Melara licence-built 68 ARVs, 28 ACEVs and 64 Armoured Vehicle, Launcher, Bridge (AVLBs).

A recent evaluation programme has studied the installation of Blohm und Voss add-on armour and a fire control system (including a thermal day/night sight) to the Italian Leopard 1 MBT, but some reports indicate that Italy plans to replace most (if not all) of them with the C-1 Ariete.

In 1977, OTO Melara and Fiat developed an export version of the Leopard 1 designated OF-40. The first prototype was ready in 1980, and in 1981 a batch of 18 OF-40 were delivered to the United Arab Emirates. A further batch of 18 OF-40 Mk. 2 were delivered (plus three ARVs), and the original batch modernised to Mk.2 standard, featuring the OG14L2A fire control system with gun stabilisation, various fire control sensors and, day/night sight and image intensification (LLLTV). The ammunition load consists of 57 rounds for the 105 mm main gun and 5,700 rounds for the 7.62 mm co-axial MG. For air defence a further 7.62 mm MG is provided, but this could optionally be replaced by a 12.7 mm HMG. The UAE proved to be the only customer for the OF-40.

After an intensive evaluation testing against the Chieftain and MBT-70, the Netherlands ordered 468 Leopard 1, which were delivered between 1969 and 1972. Many components of the Dutch version, which resembles the Leopard 1 (4th batch), were built by Dutch companies such as DAF. Unlike its German counterpart, the Leopard 1 NL was equipped with US radio sets and US style antenna bases, and was fitted out with a Dutch-designed smoke discharging system consisting of six launchers mounted in three pairs to either side of the turret. There were additional stowage boxes fitted to the sides of the hull. In lieu of the MG 3, 7.62 mm MAGs were used for secondary armament. At a later date the Leopard 1 NL received a gun stabilisation system (Honeywell) and received improved optics to fire British-designed APDS ammunition.

Meanwhile all 468 Dutch vehicles were modified with side skirts, Blohm und Voss add-on tur-

Head-on view of a Belgian Leopard 1 BE going downrange during the CAT 89 NATO tank gunnery competition. The crosswind velocity sensor of the SABCA FCS is clearly visible on the turret roof. (P-Info NORTHAG)

ret-armour and a EMES 12 A3 AFSL-2 fire control system, configured to Dutch specifications and made by Honeywell/Zeiss. The modified MBTs were designated Leopard 1 V, 'V' standing for Verbeterd (Improved), and equipped with the old, original tracks of the Diehl D139E2 type.

In the early nineties the Dutch government announced that by 1995 the Leopard 1 V MBT would be phased out of service. In early 1995, 52 ARVs, 14 AVLBs, 12 drivers training tanks and 95 PRTL air defence systems remained in operation with the Royal Netherlands Army.

In 1971, Norway took delivery of 78 Leopard 1, followed by four ARVs supplied by MaK System. Closely resembling the German Leopard 1 (4th batch), the Norwegian vehicles underwent a modernisation programme ending in 1994, when the hydraulic gun control system was replaced by an

Prototype of the improved Belgian Leopard 1 BE undergoing comparative trials with a German Leopard 1A5 in April 1989. The new FCS includes a thermal day/night sight mounted in a square housing to the right front of the turret roof. The mast with the crosswind sensor is visible above the smoke dispensers. (Michael Jerchel)

Leopard C1 of the 8th Canadian Hussars (Princess Louise's), 4th Canadian Mechanised Brigade Group, sport the widely adopted NATO camouflage pattern during live firing exercises in Bergen. The white bordered maple leaf stands out well on the turret. (Michael Jerchel)

all-electric system and EMES 18 FCS installed, bringing them up to A5-standard. A further batch of 92 Leopard 1A5 are being upgraded for the Norwegian Army. Between 1982-83, a total of 77 Leopard 1 TR were delivered to Turkey, of which 54 were built by Krauss-Maffei and 23 by MaK, plus four ARVs also built by MaK. The Leopard 1 TR is fitted with the EMES 12 A3 and mounts the PZB 200 image intensification system. Between 1990-91, a further batch of 150 former Bundeswehr MBTs (equipped with EMES 12 A3 and designated Leopard T1), were delivered. A further batch of 110 Leopard 1A1A1 (modified to A5 standard?) are thought to have been supplied to the Turkish Army under the German government's 'Armament aid' programme.

The small hatch in the left side of the welded turret allows easy reloading of ammunition or the disposal of spent casings. The 4th CMBG left Germany for Canada in 1993. (Michael Jerchel)

World-wide exports

The Australian version, designated Leopard AS 1, was chosen for the Royal Australian Armoured Corps after an intensive evaluation against the US-built M60A1 in 1973. The Leopard AS 1 is based on the German A3-version (welded turret/5th batch), but features a Belgian-designed SABCA fire control system with enhanced capabilities to fire APFSDS-T rounds, plus improved trunnion bearings, tropical kit, improved combustion cleaners and extra stowage boxes on the vehicle's sides. Between 1976 and 1978, 90 Leopard AS 1 MBTs, eight Leopard AS 1 Armoured Recovery Vehicles Medium and five Leopard AS 1 AVLBs were delivered to Australia. A small number of dozer-blades were also purchased.

The Canadian version is designated Leopard C1, some 83 and 31 vehicles being delivered by Krauss-Maffei and MaK System respectively from 1978. As part of the contract for 114 Leopard C1 MBTs, six AVLBs and eight ARVs (called Taurus

'A' Sqn commander's Leopard C1, 8th Canadian Hussars, on the Bergen firing range in March 1990. The C1 is fitted with the Belgian SABCA FCS; PZB 200 LLLTV is mounted on the gun mantlet. (Michael Jerchel)

Hydraulic dozer blades were issued to one tank per armoured squadron in the 4th CMBG. When the dozer blade is mounted, the headlights have to be repositioned. (Michael Jerchel)

in Canadian service), Krauss-Maffei agreed to purchase the entire Canadian Centurion fleet. A number of Centurion turrets (including the 105 mm guns) were subsequently ordered by Austria for static defence.

Externally the Leopard C1 is very similar to the German Leopard 1A3, but is equipped with the Belgian SABCA fire control system. In lieu of the optical stereoscopic rangefinder, it has a target acquisition sight and a laser rangefinder installed to the left side of the turret with the integrated whitelight searchlight to the right. On the mantlet to the left is a PZB 200 passive image intensification system. A 7.62 mm FN MAG (made under licence in Canada as the Minimi) is fitted for air defence (operated by the loader), a second being used as the co-axial secondary armament. Currently trials are under way to improve the main armament. In 1989 Canada placed an order for nine Badger Armoured Combat Engineer Vehicles (ACEV), the first of which was delivered by MaK System in March 1990. The Leopard C1 equipped two armoured regiments (Royal Canadian Dragoons and VIII Canadian Hussars, of which one remained stationed in Canada, and one formed part of the 4th Canadian Mechanised Brigade Group in Germany, leaving in 1993.

VARIANTS

Leopard 1 Driver Training Tank

In addition to theoretical education and simulator training, the Bundeswehr utilises 60 Leopard 1 driver tanks delivered between 1978-79 by Krauss-Maffei. The turret is replaced by an observation cabin with a dummy gun. The instructor, with appropriate devices to override the trainee driver, sits in the front seat inside the 'glasshouse'. Two additional seats are provided on either side for trainees (to observe only). Most driver tanks have the external intercom box removed from the rear plate.

Bergepanzer 2 Standard Armoured Recovery Vehicle

When development of the Standard-Panzer began (later Leopard 1) the need for a capable ARV was immediately recognised, as was the need for maximum commonality with the new MBT. Detailed design of the ARV started in 1962, headed by Porsche, and the first two prototypes built by Jung-Jungenthal were ready in 1964. After successful trials in 1965, prime contractor Krupp MaK (now MaK System) commenced

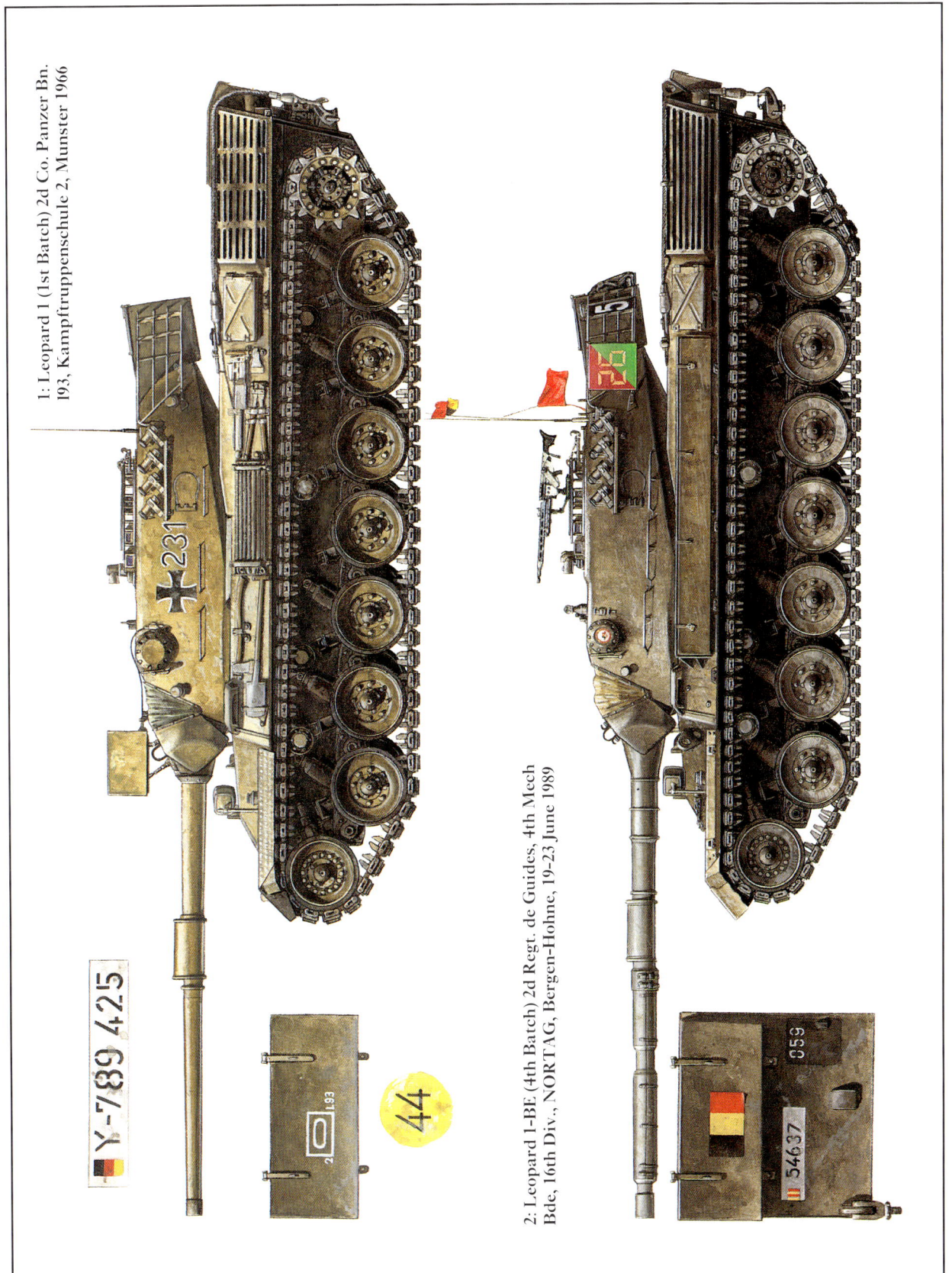

1: Leopard 1 (1st Batch) 2d Co. Panzer Bn. 193, Kampftruppenschule 2, Munster 1966

2: Leopard 1-BE (4th Batch) 2d Regt. de Guides, 4th Mech Bde, 16th Div., NORTAG, Bergen-Hohne, 19-23 June 1989

Y-731 559

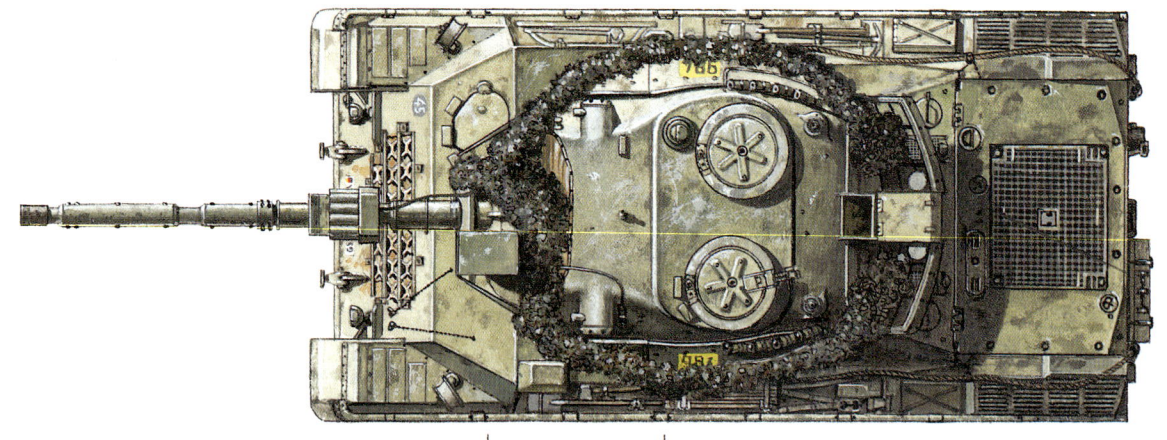

Leopard 1 A1A3, 4th Co, Panzer Bn. 354, 12th Pz Div., REFORGER FTX 'Certain Challenge', September 1988

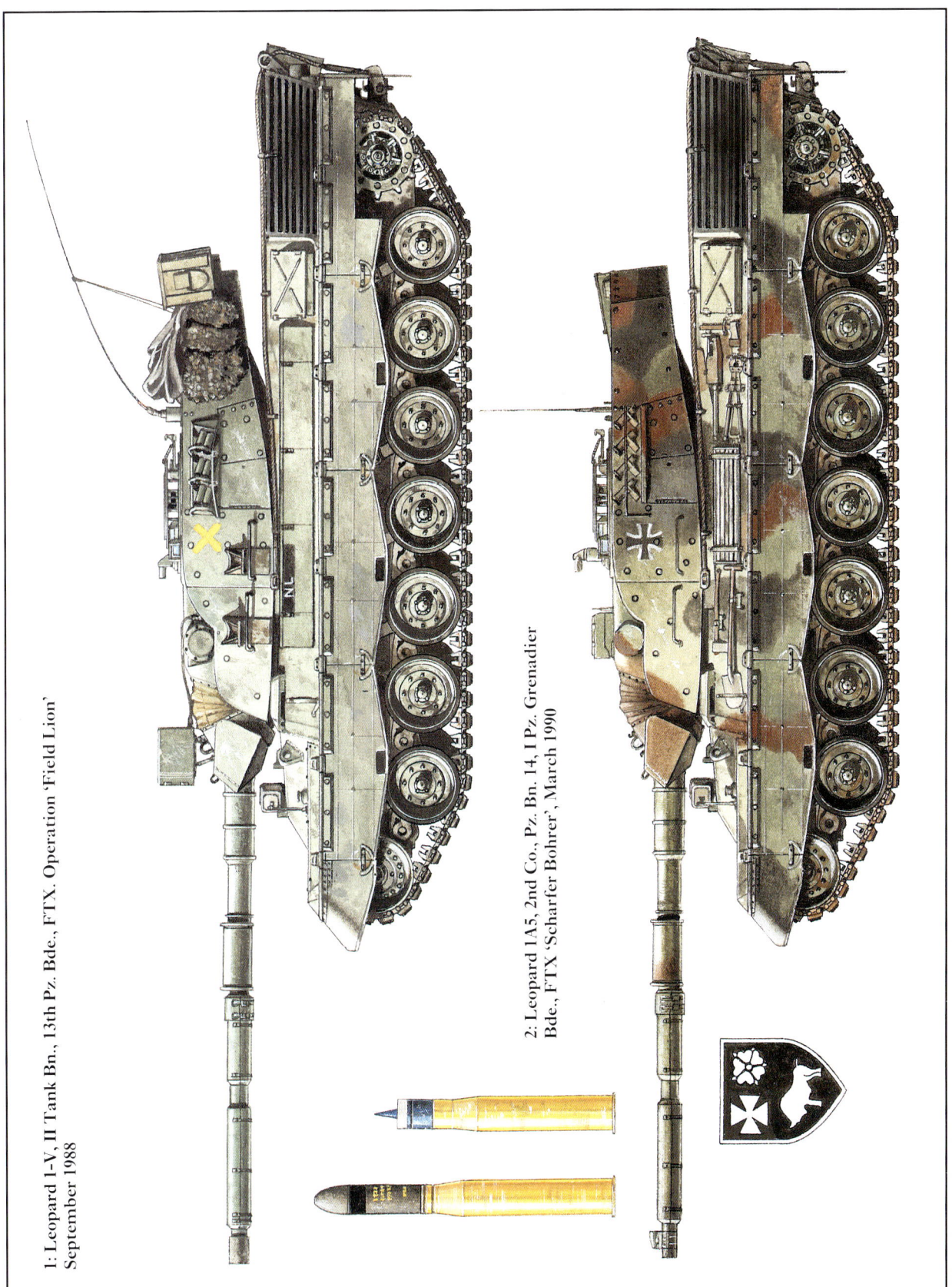

1: Leopard 1-V, II Tank Bn., 13th Pz. Bde., FTX Operation 'Field Lion' September 1988

2: Leopard 1A5, 2nd Co., Pz. Bn. 14, I Pz. Grenadier Bde., FTX 'Scharfer Bohrer', March 1990

LEOPARD 1 A1 A2
Bad Oeynhausen, late 1994

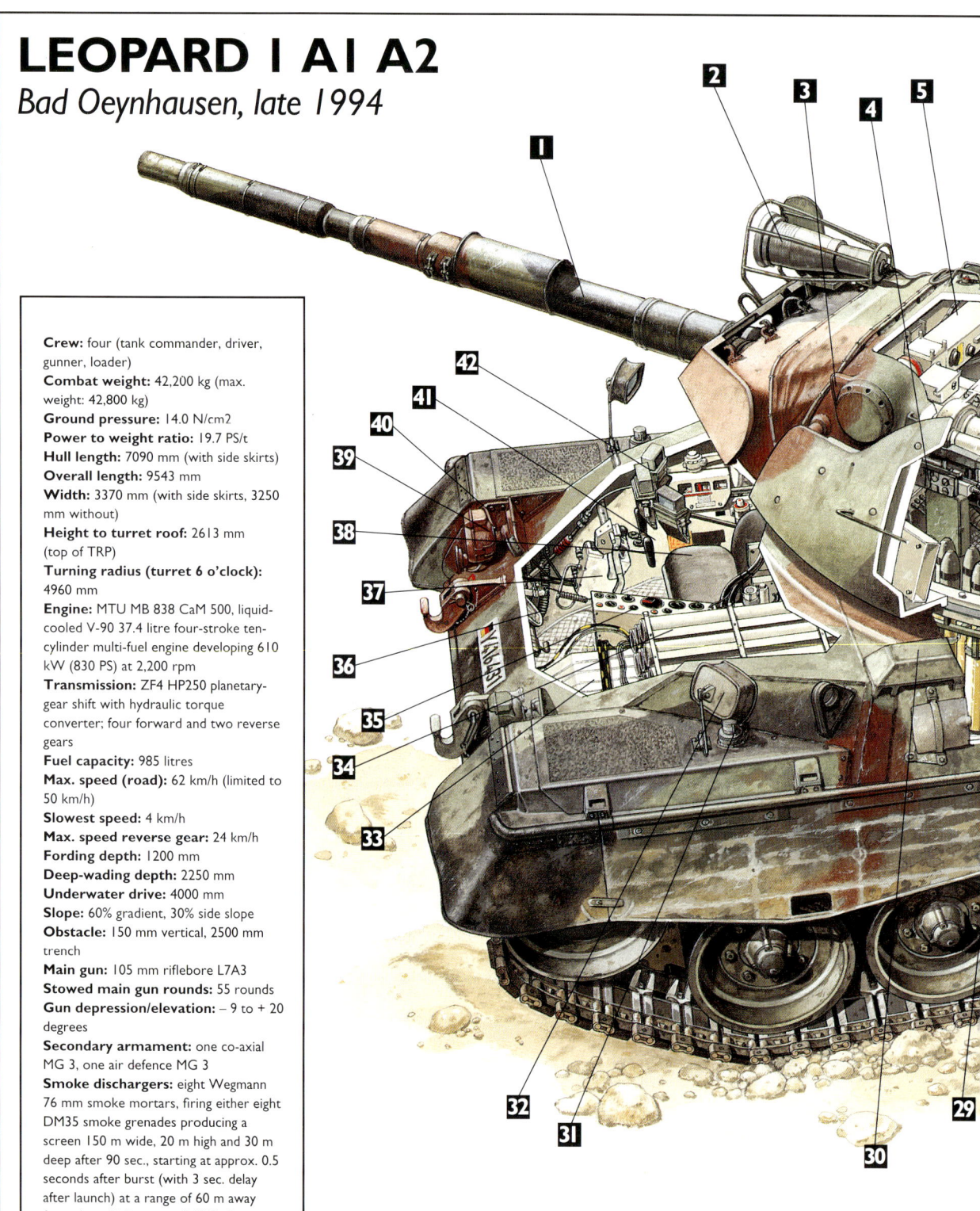

Crew: four (tank commander, driver, gunner, loader)
Combat weight: 42,200 kg (max. weight: 42,800 kg)
Ground pressure: 14.0 N/cm2
Power to weight ratio: 19.7 PS/t
Hull length: 7090 mm (with side skirts)
Overall length: 9543 mm
Width: 3370 mm (with side skirts, 3250 mm without)
Height to turret roof: 2613 mm (top of TRP)
Turning radius (turret 6 o'clock): 4960 mm
Engine: MTU MB 838 CaM 500, liquid-cooled V-90 37.4 litre four-stroke ten-cylinder multi-fuel engine developing 610 kW (830 PS) at 2,200 rpm
Transmission: ZF4 HP250 planetary-gear shift with hydraulic torque converter; four forward and two reverse gears
Fuel capacity: 985 litres
Max. speed (road): 62 km/h (limited to 50 km/h)
Slowest speed: 4 km/h
Max. speed reverse gear: 24 km/h
Fording depth: 1200 mm
Deep-wading depth: 2250 mm
Underwater drive: 4000 mm
Slope: 60% gradient, 30% side slope
Obstacle: 150 mm vertical, 2500 mm trench
Main gun: 105 mm riflebore L7A3
Stowed main gun rounds: 55 rounds
Gun depression/elevation: – 9 to + 20 degrees
Secondary armament: one co-axial MG 3, one air defence MG 3
Smoke dischargers: eight Wegmann 76 mm smoke mortars, firing either eight DM35 smoke grenades producing a screen 150 m wide, 20 m high and 30 m deep after 90 sec., starting at approx. 0.5 seconds after burst (with 3 sec. delay after launch) at a range of 60 m away from the vehicle, or six DM35 plus two fragmentation grenades Diehl M-DN21 or M-DN31. Latter have a range of approx. 45 m

D

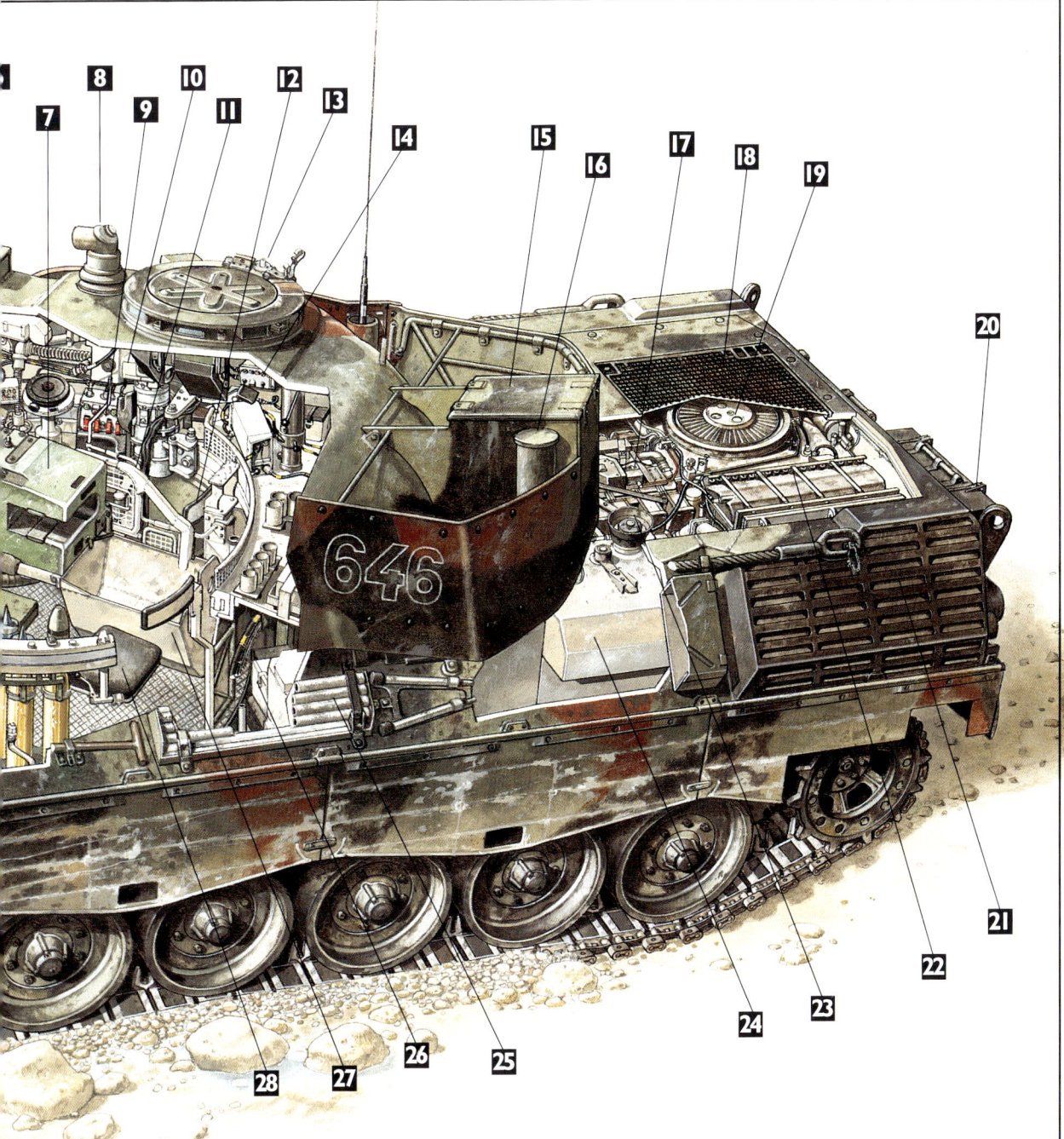

KEY

1. 105 mm L7A3 main gun
2. LLLTV camera of PZB 200
3. Left side optical head of TEM 1A
4. Co-axial 7.62 mm MG 3
5. TEM-1A coincidence sight
6. Gunner's optics of TEM 1A
7. Gun breech of L7A3 main gun
8. Commander's TRP 1A independent sight
9. Commander's electric control panel
10. Commander's TRP 1A
11. Protection around breech area
12. Commander's position
13. Air defence MG 3 mount
14. SEM 25 radio set
15. Stowage bin for searchlight
16. Stowage bin for gun cleaning devices
17. MTU MB 838 CaM 500 powerpack
18. Cooling air intake grill
19. Cooling fan assembly
20. Tool box
21. Left side exhaust grill
22. Cooling liquid reservoir/radiator
23. Fuel fitting station
24. Left side fuel tank
25. Camouflage net support struts (static use)
26. 12-volt battery
27. Ammunition casing collection bag
28. Loader's station
29. Ready use ammunition
30. Air intake for NBC system
31. Left position light
32. Left rear-view mirror
33. NBC system
34. Ammunition storage rack
35. Driver's instrument panel
36. Driver's foot pedals
37. Gearbox
38. Driver's station
39. Right headlight
40. Camouflage light
41. Driver's steering column
42. Driver's central periscope

Leopard 1 A3 (5th Batch) Pz. Auflel Bn. 10, REFORGER FTX 'Certain Challenge', September 1988

1: Leopard C-1, A-Sqd., VIII Canadian Hussars, 4th CMBG, Bergen-Hohne, March 1990

2: Leopard 1 A5-DK, DANSQN, UNPROFOR, Tuzla, Bosnia, January 1995

F

Flugabwehrpanzer 1, Gepard A1, 3rd Battery/ Air Defence Regt., Bergen Training Area, March 1993

Leopard 1 DK on the move during Exercise 'Offenes Visier' in September 1989. Due to its rough fabric construction, the camouflage matting proved difficult to decontaminate and was subsequently removed. (1st (GE) Corps)

All Danish Leopard 1 MBTs are modified to carry either the dozer blade or Tracked Width Mine Plough (TWMP). This Leopard 1A5 DK was photographed at the Danish Armour School (HKS) in May 1994. (Andreas Kirchhoff)

Dutch Leopard 1 V of Tankbataljon 11 participates in a river crossing operation during Exercise 'Free Lion' in September 1988. A searchlight is mounted to the 7.62 mm FN MAG at the loader's station and a Dutch-designed gunfire simulator is attached to the mantlet near the gun barrel. (Michael Jerchel)

series production of the Bergepanzer 2 Standard, the first vehicle of 444 built being delivered in September 1966. Bergepanzer 2 replaced the obsolete M74 and a number of M88s.

Bergepanzer 2 shares a 75 per cent parts commonalty with the Leopard 1 MBT, and has a hull of all-welded construction. The driver sits in the front, a hatch opening to the left; three vision periscopes are provided. The commander is situated behind the driver's station has has eight periscopes. Space and provisions are available for two mechanics: one is seated to the left of the driver to operate the 7.62 mm MG 3 in a ball bearing mount, installed to the front left in the glacis plate; the other is seated behind the commander and has a separate hatch, which opens to the left, and three vision periscopes facing to the rear. Two doors to the left side of the hull allow easy access to the interior of the ARV. A further 7.62 mm MG 3 is fitted to the commander's cupola for air defence. Mounted on the left side of the hull is a smoke dispensing system with six smoke mortars attached to it.

The main winch is installed inside the ARV, below the floor of the crew compartment. The opening for the 33 mm thick winch cable, with a total length of 90 m, is situated in the bow. The opening is protected by a sliding hatch, opening to the left for operation. The maximum tow load is 350 kN (35,000 kg), which can be doubled when using a guide block pulley. Latter is carried on the bow when not in use. A secondary winch is provided, also installed inside the vehicle. The winch cable is 13 mm in diameter has a maximum length of 100 m, and is able to pull a maximum of 200 kN (20,000 kg), which can be increased to 350 kN by multi-reeving (x6) the cable.

The dozer blade is lowered and raised by two

A company of Dutch Leopard 1-V on the march during exercise 'Free Lion' in September 1988. The tanks are of 11th Tank Battalion and play the enemy, hence the yellow crosses on the tanks. (Michael Jerchel)

hydraulic cylinders and is used as a support to stabilise the ARV for winching or crane operations. The hydraulic crane is mounted to the right side at the vehicle's front. When not in use, the crane is lowered and, pointing rearward, rests along the hull. For operation the crane jib is raised and can be traversed hydraulically through 270° (max. load 130 kN). If the hydraulics fail, it can be operated manually. Using the dozer blade for stabilisation, the crane is able to lift a maximum load of 200 kN (20,000 kg).

The engine compartment is at the rear, Bergepanzer 2 utilising the same powerpack and transmission system as the Leopard 1 MBT. Bergepanzer 2 has a combat weight of 39,800 kg and is capable of 62 km/h; range is 850 km on roads and 500 km cross country. Eventually 104 Bergepanzer 2 Standard of the entire fleet were converted into Pionierpanzer 2 Dachs (Badger).

This close up of a Leopard 1 V turret shows the Dutch smoke dispensing system to either side and the US style antenna sockets, the two chocks for which are stowed in the turret guard rails. (Michael Jerchel)

35

Like most Norwegian Leopards, this snow white example has an extra stowage box on the upper glacis plate. A gunfire simulator is mounted on the gun barrel. (Norwegian MoD)

Pionierpanzer 1 Armoured Combat Engineer Vehicle

In 1966 the need for a special ACEV was acknowledged, the vehicle being duly designed by Porsche. MaK was appointed prime contractor and the first prototype began trials in 1967, series production of 36 vehicles for the Bundeswehr commencing one year later. Officially designated Bergepanzer 2A1, the vehicle is based on the ARV and special equipment includes an auger, stored on the engine deck, fitted to the crane jib and hydraulically operated. The Pionierpanzer 1 is also equipped with electric cutting and welding equipment. The crane jib incorporates a ladder. The PiPz 1 can carry 117 kg of explosives for demolition work. Attachments can extend the dozer blade to a width of 3.75 m, giving the vehicle a dozing capacity of 200 cub.m/h. Four scarifiers may be mounted to the rear of the dozer. In addition, the PiPz is also a fully capable ARV, having a guide block pulley stored on the bow. All 36 Pionierpanzer 1 in German service were converted into Pionierpanzer 2 Dachs (Badger).

Bergepanzer 2A2 Armoured Recovery Vehicle

Following demands of units equipped with the Leopard 2 and Gepard for an increased lifting capability, in 1978 MaK System delivered 100 improved ARVs. The Bergepanzer 2A2 received support struts at the rear right, which relieves the ARV's right side and now allows a max. load of 160 kN (16,000 kg) to be traversed within 270°. The max. lifting load of 200 kN remained unchanged, although lifting height was also increased by this improvement. The separate circular base plate is stored on the left side of the hull when not in use, and the support strut is swung up. Improvements included an enhanced NBC protection system. The combat weight of the Bergepanzer 2A2 increased to 40,585 kg.

Pionierpanzer 2 Dachs Armoured Combat Engineer Vehicle

After developments of the Gepanzerte Pioniermaschine (GPM) armoured engineer vehicle were dropped due to financial and weight problems, the Office of Development and Procurement (BWB) devised a low-cost solution and from 1981 to 1985 the Pionierpanzer 2 Dachs was developed. MaK System of Kiel was awarded the production/conversion contract. On 13 April 1989 the first series vehicle of 140 ordered was handed over to Bundeswehr.

The PiPz 2 Dachs were converted from 36 PiPz 1 and 104 Bergepanzer 2, which were stripped down completely and then had the new compo-

Bergepanzer 2 Standard ARV during winching operations, for which a cable emerges through the aperture provided, covered by a sliding door opening to the left, as seen here. *The main winch is installed below the floor of the crew compartment. (Michael Jerchel)*

Dutch Bergingtank ARV with a YPR-765 PRAT in tow and a spare engine (protected by a tarpaulin) on the engine deck. The Dutch version of the Leopard ARV, seen here during FTX 'Offenes Visier' in 1989, retains the original track configuration. (Michael Jerchel)

The improved Leopard ARV, Bergepanzer 2A2, incorporates support struts, seen here in the travelling position on this vehicle of Panzerbataillon 33.(Michael Jerchel)

nents built in. Instead of the original crane an hydraulically powered telescopic excavator arm was fitted, operated by remote control and traversings 195°. The excavating capacity is 140 cub.m/h. A new hydraulic system was installed, working on a constant pressure of 300 bar. The Dachs has an integral 50 volt-generator for the on-board welding and cutting equipment. The dozer blade at the vehicle's bow has 'built-in' side extensions, which allow an increase in width to 3.750 mm, and two scarifiers are mounted to the rear of the dozer blade.

The periscopes for the driver and on the commander's cupola were increased in height so as to ensure an uninteruptedview of the excavator when operating under armour. The Dachs can work in water up to 2.25 m deep; improved bilge pumps were built in. A 7.62 mm MG 3 can be fitted to the commander's cupola for air defence, and six mortars form the smoke dispensing system installed to the left side of the hull. The combat weight of the Dachs is 43,000 kg.

Brückenlegepanzer 1 Biber Bridgelayer

The development programme for a bridgelayer based on a modified Leopard 1 chassis started in 1965, and in 1969 two prototypes were ready. The one of Group A vehicle laid the bridge using a telescopic boom, while the one from Group B was of the cantilever type. The latter was chosen for series production, with MaK as prime contractor. The first of 105 Brückenlegepanzer 1 Biber (Beaver) AULB were delivered in 1975.

The Biber has a crew of two, the driver sitting in the front and the commander in a central position offset to the right. The hull of the vehicle was slightly increased in length due to the addition of a new battery compartment now provided at the rear. The total length of the Biber with

Although officially designated Bergepanzer 2A1, the armoured combat engineer vehicle (ACEV), became known as the Pionierpanzer 1. Normally stowed on the bow, the guide block pulley is seen here in position for increased winching capability. (Michael Jerchel)

Bergepanzer 2A2 ARV in the process of changing the powerpack of a Leopard 2A4 MBT. The base plate for the support struts at the rear is stored on the left side of the hull, and a spare wheel is carried on the rear deck. (Michael Jerchel)

39

When Germany participated in the UN mission to Somalia (UNOSOM), the sole ARV to accompany the force was this Bergepanzer 2A2, seen on its return at Emden harbour in March 1994. (Michael Jerchel)

bridge is 11.82 m (w/o bridge 10.56 m).

The MLC 60 bridge is made of aluminium, 4 m wide, and carried in two 11 m halves, one above the other. To launch the bridge, the Biber lowers the small support blade on the bow, which could also be used for limited dozing operations prior to the bridge launching operation. The lower half of the bridge slides forward until it can be coupled with the upper half. Then both sections are coupled together, before the bridge is extended over the gap, lowered into position and the cantilever arm withdrawn. The bridge can span gaps up to 20 m wide, and can be taken up from either side. On the rear jib eight smoke mortars are fitted, the only self-defence available. Gross weight (including the bridge) is 45,300 kg.

Flugabwehrpanzer 1 Gepard and PRTL Anti-Aircraft Vehicle

In 1965 a development programme was started for a new self-propelled air defence gun system for the Bundeswehr to replace the fair weather M42. After evaluating prototypes of the Matador with 30 mm twin guns (developed by Rheinmetall, AEG, Siemens and Krauss-Maffei) and the competing 5PFZ-A with 35 mm twin guns (built and delivered in 1968 by a consortium made up by Oerlikon, Contraves, Siemens-Albis, Hollandse-Signaalapparaten and Krauss-Maffei/Porsche), it was decided to concentrate on the latter design. In 1971 a further four trial vehicles were delivered with the designation 5PZF-B, which had their Dutch radar systems replaced with German radars made by Siemens. A pre-series batch of 12 5PZF-B1 with the MPDR-12 radar was ordered and delivered in 1973.

In September 1973 an order for 420 Flugabwehrpanzer 1 Gepard was placed for the Bundeswehr, which were delivered between 1976 and 1980 by Krauss-Maffei. After the first 195 vehicles, known as the (5PZF-) B2 and designated Flakpanzer 1 Gepard, were delivered, the remaining 225 were fitted with a Siemens laser rangefinder on top of the tracking radar radome installed to the turret front and are known as the (5PZF-) B2L, designated Flakpanzer 1 Gepard A1. The Gepard has a modified Leopard 1 hull designed by Porsche and manufactured by Krauss-Maffei. The hull between the 3rd and 4th road wheel station was increased by 80mm, and the first, second, third, fifth, sixth and seventh wheel station received a hydraulic shock absorber. The track has 85 track links (compared to 84 on the Leopard 1). A DB OM-314 auxiliary power unit (APU) with a max. output of 66 kW (90 PS) is installed to the left of the driver, the exhaust running along the left side of the hull to the rear. The air-inlet for the APU and the NBC protection system is installed on the vehicle's upper glacis to the left. At the rear of the hull was a new compartment for a set of six batteries.

The turret has twin Oerlikon-Bührle 35 mm KDA L/R04 35/90 guns with a cyclic rate of 550 rounds per minute each. A MPDR-12 pulse Doppler surveillance radar, working in the E/F-bands, and MSR 400 IFF system made by Siemens, is installed to the turret rear. The radar rotates at 60 rpm and has a range of 15 km.

When the MPDR-12 surveillance radar has picked up a target and the IFF system identifies it as hostile, the pulse Doppler tracking radar made by Siemens-Albis installed to the turret front takes over. Normally stored facing the front of the turret, it traverses 180° for operation, having a range of 15 km and tracking the target automatically in azimuth, elevation and range (the Gepard A1 also has a laser rangefinder). The analogue fire control computer, made by Contraves, calculates the lead angles based on all the relevant fire control data. When the target is within range (about 4000 m), the Gepard opens fire.

The commander sits to the left in the turret and the gunner to the right. Both have a fully stabilised panoramic sight, mounted in the turret roof to the front of their stations. The sights can be slaved to the tracking radar or used for optical target acquisition of either air or ground targets. The commander is provided with an optical target indicator when working in the open hatch. Ammunition load is 620 rounds (HEI-T, SAPHEI-T, APDS-T or TP-T) split equally between each gun. In addition, 40 rounds of anti-

Pionierpanzer 2 Dachs ACEV fitted with a deep wading snorkel, allowing it to work in the water to a max. depth of 2.25 m. The remote control set may be seen in front of the commander, standing in the snorkel. (Michael Jerchel)

Included in the German UNOSOM in Somalia were two Pionierpanzer 2 Dach ACEVs; this one was photographed on return to Emden. (Michael Jerchel)

tank ammunition is carried under armour at the gun breeches for self-defence against hostile AFVs (and other ground targets) should the need arise.

Gepards are currently being modified with an optronic sensor that allows the radars to remain inactivated during (passive) search, surveillance and tracking. The new digital fire control computer is a major advance, enhancing hit probability even against highly manoeuvrable targets. B2 Gepards will be fitted with a laser rangefinder to bring them up to B2L Gepard A1-standard.

41

One of the new UN Pionierpanzer 2 Dachs after return from the UNOSOM mission at Emden harbour. Both vehicles saw extensive service in Somalia, including road building tasks. (Michael Jerchel)

A Brückenlepanzer 'Biber' of Pz.Co. 40, showing the two 11m halves of the bridge to good advantage. (M.Jerchel)

The Belgian Army currently has 55 Gepards in service, which were delivered between the period covering 1977 and 1980, and are equivalent to the German B2 version.

The first prototype of the Dutch version, designated 5PFZ-C, was ready in 1969, having the radar designed by Hollandse Signaalapparaten (HSA) installed. In 1971 a pre-series of five vehicles were delivered, which had a reworked turret rear for the Dutch radar designated 5PZF-CA. Delivery of the 95 series vehicles, known as 5PZF-CA1 and designated PRTL (Pantser Rups Tegen Luchtdoelen) by the Royal Netherlands Army, started in 1977. The PRTL is easily recognised by the T-shaped surveillance radar, but with the original D139E2 tracks with modified chassis.

THE PLATES

Plate A-1: *Leopard 1 (1st batch), 2nd Company, Panzerlehrbataillon 93, Kampftruppenschule 2, Munster 1966*

The Panzerlehrbataillon was the first Panzerbataillon (raised on 1 April 1956) of the Bundeswehr. Following Structure 59, the battalion number '93' was added to differentiate it from the Panzerlehrbataillon 94 (formed in 1960). Under command of Kampftruppenschule (KTS) 2, the German armour school, PzBtl. L93 carried out most of the trials with the prototypes and the pre-series vehicles. It was the first unit to receive the series production Leopard 1 of the first batch in late 1965, and provided initial training for officers and NCOs of other Panzerbatallions before these were equipped with the new MBT. The inset shows the new rectangular shaped tactical marking, denoting 2nd Company of Armour Training Battalion 93 (PzBtl. L93), which was introduced shortly after the new tank had come into service. The black '44' on yellow roundel, applied to the right on the upper glacis plate, denotes military loading class (MLC). The registration plate was carried on the upper glacis and, at this time, on the tool box to the left side of the rear plate.

Plate A-2: *Leopard 1 BE, 2ème Régiment de Guides, 4th Mechanised Brigade, 16th Division, Northern Army Group Team, CAT 89 competition, Bergen-Hohne, 19-23 June 1989*

The Belgian Army was the first foreign customer for the new MBT, the first Leopard 1 BE entering service in 1968. Apart from minor modifications – from 1975 stowage boxes were fitted to the vehicle's sides and the main gun received a thermal sleeve – the external appearance of the Leopard 1 BE remained largely unchanged until the mid-1990s. In June 1989 the Leopard 1 BE of 2 Gidsen (as the unit is known in Flemish) participated in the prestigious Canadian Army Trophy (CAT) tank gunnery competition held on range 9 at the NATO exercise area in Bergen. The Belgian crews, the only unit of the NORTHAG CAT-team with the Leopard 1, acknowledged the

Gepard A1 self-propelled anti-aircraft gun (SPAAG) of Flugabwehr Regiment 2 on the march during an exercise in 1993, with the surveillance radar at the turret rear lowered. Red crosses denote the vehicle as part of the opposing forces (OPFOR). (Michael Jerchel)

similarly equipped Canadian team of CENTAG as their main opponents. The trophy was won by NORTHAG (the first six platoons of which were equipped with the Leopard 2). The NATO CAT competition was held every two years, alternating between Bergen and Grafenwöhr ranges, between Northern Army Group (NORTHAG) and Central Army Group (CENTAG). Inset is the Belgian flag applied for CAT 89, and the licence plates carried on the glacis and rear plate.

Plate B: *Leopard 1A1A3, 4th Company, Panzerbataillon 354, 12th Panzer Division, REFORGER FTX 'Certain Challenge', September 1988*

From 1979, when the Leopard 2 began to re-equip the armoured battalions within the Panzer brigades, the Leopard 1 was re-deployed to the armoured battalions within the Panzer grenadier brigades. This Leopard 1A1A3 participated in the last major REFORGER field training exercise (FTX) ever held, conducted in September 1988 as 'Certain Challenge'. The tank has a gunfire simulator (Hoffman-device) fitted to the gun barrel and the searchlight is mounted on the mantlet. Although equipped with the new SEM 80/90 radios (as indicated by their short antennae) and therefore designated an A1A3, the tank retains its olive green (RAL 6014) paint scheme. The turret number '456' on the rear add-on armour denotes a vehicle of the 4th company, while the black '984' on a yellow square is a unit identification number unique to this exercise. A large camouflage net is draped around the turret to break up its shape. Inset is the vehicle licence plate and the badge of Panzerbataillon 354 carried on the bin at the turret rear, to the left of which is the non-standard attachment added by this unit for an extra fuel can. Panzerbataillon 354 of Panzer grenadier brigade 35 operated in support of Kampftruppenschule 1, the German infantry school, in Hammelburg.

Plate C-1: *Leopard 1 V, 11 Tank Bataljon, 13 Pantser Brigade, (NL) Division 1 '7 Dezember', FTX 'Free Lion', September 1988*

The Dutch Leopard 1 MBTs fitted with Blohm und Voss add-on armour and EMES 12 A3 AFSL-2 are designated Leopard 1 V (Verbeterd, i.e. improved). The 13th Armoured Brigade was formed in 1979 at Oirschot, the Netherlands. The yellowish-green crosses denote that this vehicle is part of the 'aggressor force from Greenland' dur-

Manned and ready, this Flakpanzer 1 Gepard A1 has the hatch open and the tracking radar swung round in the operating position. The exhaust for the APU runs along the left side of the hull. (Michael Jerchel)

ing Exercise 'Free Lion', held by Ist (NL) Corps in September 1988. On the small black bar applied to the first stowage boxes on either side (and the bow) are for the chalked marching orders added after the two painted letters: 'NL' for vehicles stationed in the Netherlands, or 'GE' for Germany.

The inset shows two examples from the broad selection of ammunition compatible with 105 mm L7A3 main gun. To the left is the M393A2 High Explosive Practice-Tracer (HEP-T) of US origin, made under licence by MECAR of Belgium. Overall length of the round is 940 mm and the muzzle velocity 730 m/s. On the right is the L50A2BG Target Practice-Tracer/Discarding Sabot (TP-T/DS) round of British origin, also used by the Belgian Army. Other user countries of the Leopard 1 produced their own selection of ammunition or used various different types, with the AP(FS)DS being the prime ammunition for engaging enemy MBTs; in the case of the Dutch Leopard 1 V, this was the British L64 round.

Plate C-2: *Leopard 1A5, IIIrd Platoon, 2nd Co., Panzerbatallion 14, Panzergrenadierbrigade 1, 1st Panzer Div. attached to 2nd Co., Panzergrenadierbataillon 12 during FTX 'Scharfer Bohrer', Bergen, March 1990.*

The EMES 18 fire control system was fitted to a certain number of the first four production batches of Bundeswehr Leopard 1 MBTs, regardless the particular batch. This vehicle was built in 1970 as part of the fourth batch. A mix of different batches within a platoon (consisting of four tanks) was common. In this case there were two Leopard 1A5s of former third batch and one of former first batch in addition to the platoon leader's tank shown, forming the IIIrd Platoon of the 2nd Company of PzBtl. 14. The vehicle sports the camouflage scheme (known as Fleckentarnanstrich, FTA) developed by the Bundeswehr, consisting of bronze-green (RAL 6031), leather-brown (RAL 8027) and tar-black (RAL 9021). These colours were later adopted by some other NATO countries, including the USA, and with the latter the colours are known as green (FS 34094), brown (FS 30051) and black (FS 37030). The inset shows the badge of Panzerbataillon 14, formerly stationed in Hildesheim (near Hannover). It was disbanded in

Gepard A1 on the march with surveillance radar lowered during REFORGER FTX 'Certain Challenge' in September 1988. The gap between the 3rd and 4th road-wheel station due to the lengthened hull is shown to advantage; Gepard is not fitted with side skirts. (PAO USAREUR)

late 1993 following German military reorganisation.

Plate D: *Leopard 1A1A2, Bad Oeynhausen, November 1994*

This particular Leopard 1 (Werke Nr. 6019) languished in a depot before being overhauled in December 1989 at Ischendorf, where the tank was brought up to A1A2 standard. It then served with the Erprobungsstelle 71 (proving ground) in Cologne, before arriving at the Motor-Technica-Museum in Bad Oeynhausen, where it is now on public display.

Plate E: *Leopard 1A3, Panzer-aufklärungs-bataillon 10, REFORGER FTX 'Certain Challenge', September 1988*

After the introduction of Leopard 2 in the Panzer brigades, the Leopard 1 was used in the armoured battalion within each Panzer grenadier brigade and within the divisional armoured reconnaissance battalion, in this case the 10th (GE) Panzer Division. The vehicle retains its plain olive green (RAL 6014) paint scheme and has no extra camouflage, rather unusual during an exercise. It was part of BLUEFOR, as denoted by the blue sign on the turret, with the unit number '901' in black. In an exercise the registration plate and tactical markings are either covered with mud or taped over for camouflage reasons. However, only a handful of Bundeswehr Leopard 1A3 MBTs received the new camouflage scheme before they were phased out of service and sold.

Plate F-1: *Leopard C1, 'A' Sqdn, VIIIth Canadian Hussars (Princess Louise's), 4th CMBG, Bergen-Hohne, March 1990*

The 4th Canadian Mechanised Brigade Group, part of Canadian Forces Europe (CFE), included the VIIIth Canadian Hussars (Princess Louise's), which alternated its commitment of one armoured battalion with the Royal Canadian Dragoons. VIIIth CH was organised in three armoured squadrons ('A', 'B' and 'C'), all of which were equipped with the Leopard C1 MBT. In about 1989, the first vehicles were repainted in NATO camouflage pattern during their normal periodic overhaul. This Leopard C1 is the 'A' Sqdn

Dutch PRTL SPAAG with tracking radar in operating mode. The PRTL's radar system was produced by Hollandse Signaalapparaten. The PRTL is occasionally referred to as the 'Cheetah', probably due to its company designator, CA1. (Michael Jerchel)

leader's tank, denoted by the black '1' carried on the vehicle sides and on the rear tool box. Inset is the marking for the 2nd platoon leader's tank of 'B' Sqn, denoted by the number '22' (platoon leaders in 'A' and 'C' Sqns were numbered '12' and '32' respectively). The tactical marking of the armoured battalion of 4th CMBG is also carried. In 1993 Canadian Forces Europe, including the 4th CMBG, returned to Canada.

Plate F-2: *Leopard 1A5 DK, DANSQN, UNPROFOR, Tuzla, Bosnia, January 1995*

The Danish Squadron of UNPROFOR had a rather frustrating and protracted journey to Tuzla airfield in Bosnia. In autumn 1993 the Danish Squadron (DANSQN), consisting of ten Leopard 1A5 DK (three with dozer-blade and three with TWMP), one Bergepanzer 2 AVLB (bought from the Netherlands) and four M113 APCs, went by train from Oksböl (Haerenskampskole, the Danish armour school) to Pancevo, near Beograd/Serbia. Serbian intransigence soon blocked attempts by DANSQN to depart for Tuzla as planned. In January 1994, the entire force was reloaded on the train and went from Pancevo via Hungary and Austria to Triest in Italy, from where it sailed via ferry to Split. DANSQN then continued on its way by road from Split via Tommyslaw, Gornii Vakuf, Vitez and Vares to Tuzla. Swedish tank transports (Scania R 143E 6 x 4 with HAFO four-axle trailers), took the armour as far as they could, but due to appalling road conditions (not to mention several tunnels, which would have involved unloading the tanks to gain adequate height clearance), the final 100 km of this odyssey had to be completed on tracks, arriving at their 'objective in February 1994.

During their deployment, one Leopard 1A5 DK reportedly fired two 105 mm rounds at a Serbian 40 mm gun, destroying it. In another incident, incoming fire from light infantry weapons, fired from fortified Serbian positions, was answered with several rounds. For service with UNPRO-

PRTL with tracking radar in stored position, facing the turret front. The HSA surveillance radar is sometimes called the 'dog bone' due to its shape. This PRTL took part in Exercise 'Certain Shield' in September 1991, hence the yellow patch (denoting 'Gold forces') on the side skirts. (Michael Jerchel)

FOR in Tuzla/Bosnia, the Danish Leopard 1A5 DKs mounted halogen searchlights 'loaned' from the M41 DK 1 light tank on the mantlet. The area immediately in front of the EMES 18 housing is painted black in order to stop reflections from confusing the gunner's sight. Most of the tanks carried an additional stowage box, 'borrowed' from an old Danish truck, on the turret rear as shown in the inset. In addition to its UN markings, this vehicle carries a Danish flag on the right side of the mantlet and on the rear tool box. The black '47' on a yellow circle is the bridge mark (MLC).

Plate G: *Flugabwehrpanzer 1 Gepard A1, 3rd Battery, Air Defence Regiment 2, Bergen Training Area, Heeresübung 93, March 1993*

Otherwise known as the B2L, the FlaPz 1 Gepard A1 is equipped with a laser rangefinder installed on top of the tracking radar radome at the turret front, shown here traversed and ready for action. During 'Heeresübung 1993' held in Bergen, FlaRgt. 2 was attached to FlaRgt. 12 – the divisional air defence unit of the 12th (GE) Panzer Division – as part of the OPFOR (opposing forces), denoted by the red crosses applied to the turret sides and the Gepard's bow. Inset is the tactical marking of 3rd Battery, Flugabwehrregiment 2 (Air Defence Regiment 2), applied to the left side of the upper glacis and on the rear plate. The number to the left of the tactical marking denotes the individual battery, while those to the right denote the regiment (or battalion). Also shown is the badge of Air Defence Regiment 2, which was stationed (and subsequently deactivated) at Kassel.

Notes sur les planches en couleur

A1 Le Panzerlehrbataillon fut le premier Panzerbataillon (levé le 1er avril 1956) du Bundeswehr. Les nouvelles marques tactiques rectangulaires, qui indiquent qu'il s'agit de la 2ème Compagnie du Bataillon de Formation des Blindés 93 PzBtl. L93, furent introduites peu après l'entrée en service du char. Le '44' noir sur un tourteau jaune, appliqué en haut à droite du parement, indique qu'il s'agit d'une classe de charge militaire (MLC). La plaque minéralogique était placée sur le parement supérieur et, à cette période, sur la boîte à outils à gauche de la plaque arrière. A2 L'armée belge fut le premier client étranger à acheter le nouveau MBT, le premer Leopard IBE entrant en service en 1968. A l'exception de quelques modifications mineures : à compter de 1975, les casiers de munitions furent installés sur les côtés du véhicule et le

47

canon principal fut équipé d'un manchon isolant, l'apparence extérieure du Leopard IBE resta pratiquement la même jusqu'au milieu des années 90. En encadré, le drapeau belge utilisé pour CAT 89 et les plaques minéralogiques du parement et de la plaque arrière.

B Ce char est doté d'un simulateur de tir au canon (dispositif Hoffman) installé sur le baril du canon et le projecteur est monté sur le mantelet. Bien qu'équipé des nouvelles radios SEM 80/90 (identifiées par leur courte antenne) et donc nommé A1A3, ce char conserve sa couleur olive (RAL 6014). La tourelle numéro '456' sur le blindage arrière amovible indique qu'il s'agit d'un véhicule de la 4ème compagnie alors que le '984' noir sur carré jaune est un numéro d'identification d'unité spécifique à cet exercice. Un grand filet de camouflage est drapé autour de la tourelle pour déguiser sa forme. En encadré, la plaque minéralogique du véhicule et le badge du Panzerbataillon 354 porté sur le casier à l'arrière de la tourelle. A sa gauche se trouve un élément non-standard ajouté par cette unité comme réservoir de carburant supplémentaire.

C1 Les Leopard I MBT néerlandais équipés du blindage Blohm und Voss amovible et les EMES 12 A3 ASFL-2 sont nommés Leopard 1 V (Verbeterd, c'est-à-dire amélioré). Les croix vert-jaune montrent que ce véhicule fait partie des 'forces d'agression du Groenland' durant les manoeuvres 'Free Lion' organisées par le 1er Corps (NL) en septembre 1988. L'encadré illustre deux exemples du grand choix de munitions compatibles avec le canon principal 105mm L7A3. A gauche se trouve un traçant explosif M393A2 (HEP-T) et à droite une cartouche d'entraînement au tir/sabot L50A2BG (TP-T/DS) d'origine britannique, également utilisé par l'armée belge. **C2** Ce véhicule porte le camouflage (connu sous le nom de Fleckentarnanstrich, FTA) mis au point par le Bundeswehr, composé de vert bronze (RAL 6031), marron-cuir (RAL 8027) et noir goudron (RAL 9021). Ces couleurs furent par la suite adoptées par d'autres pays membres de l'OTAN, y compris les Etats-Unis et dans ce dernier le nom de ces couleurs est vert (FS 34094), marron (FS 30051) et noir (FS 37030). L'encadré montre le badge du Panzerbataillon 14, anciennement stationné à Hildesheim (près de Hanovre).

D Ce Leopard I (Werke Nr. 6019) se languissait dans un dépôt avant d'être rénové en décembre 1989 à Ischendorf où l'on amena ce char au niveau A1 A2. Il fut ensuite mis en service àErprobungsstelle 71 (terrain d'essai) à Cologne, avant de finir au Motor-Technica-Museum à Bad Oeynhausen, où il est maintenant exposé.

E Leopard I, 10ème (GE) Division Panzer. Ce véhicule conserve sa couleur vert olive (RAL 6014) et ne possède aucun camouflage supplémentaire, ce qui est assez inhabituel durant des manoeuvres. Il faisait partie de BLUEFOR, ce qui est indiqué par la marque bleue sur la tourelle, accompagné du numéro de l'unité, '901' en noir. Néanmoins, seulement une poignée de Bundeswehr Leopard 1A3 MTB reçurent le nouveau type de camouflage avant de les retirer progressivement et de les vendre.

F1 Le 4ème Groupe de Brigade Canadien Mécanisé, qui faisait parte des Forces Canadiennes Europe (CFE). Vers 1989, les premiers véhicules furent repeints selon le motif de camouflage de l'OTAn durant leur révision normale. Ce Leopard C2 est le char du chef d'escadron 'A', comme l'indique le 'I' noir sur les côtés du véhicule et sur la boîte à outils arrière. En encadré, nous avons la marque du char du chef de train de l'escadron 'B', dénoté par le numéro '22' (les chefs de train des escadrons 'A' et 'C' avaient le numéro 12 et 32 respectivement). Les marques tactiques du bataillon blindé du 4ème CMBG sont également incluses. **F2** En automne 1993, l'escadron danois (DANSQN) était composé de dix Leopard 1A5 DK (trois avec lame niveleuse et trois avec TWMP), un Bergepanzer 2 AVLB (achetés aux Pays-Bas) et quatre APC M113. A part les marques des Nations Unies, ce véhicule porte un drapeau danois sur la droite du mantelet et sur la boîte à outils arrière. Le '47' noir sur un cercle jaune est la marque pont (MLC).

G Le FlaPz I Gepard A1, également connu sous le nom de B2L, est équipé d'un colimateur laser installé sur le dessus du dôme radar à l'arrière de la tourelle, illustrée ici en position et prête à l'action. En encadré nous avons les marques tactiques de la 3ème batterie, Flugabwehrregiment 2 (Régiment de défense aérienne 2), appliqué sur la gauche du parement supérieur et sur la plaque arrière. Le numéro à gauche de la marque tactique dénote la batterie alors que les numéros sur la droite indiquent le régiment (ou bataillon). Egalement illustré, le badge du Régiment de défense aérienne 2, qui fut stationné (et par la suite désactivé) à Kassel.

Farbtafeln

A1 Das Panzerlehrbataillon war das erste Panzerbataillon der Bundeswehr, das den neuen Leopard erhielt. Das neue, rechteckige taktische Zeichen - hier bezeichnet es die 2. Kompanie des Panzerlehrbataillon 93 (PzBtl. L93) - wurde kurze Zeit später eingeführt. Die schwarze Ziffer "44" auf gelbem Kreis, auf der rechten oberen Seite der Bugplatte angebracht, kennzeichnet die militärische Lastenklasse (MLC). Das Kennzeichen war mittig auf der oberen Bugplatte und, zu dieser Zeit, auf dem Werkzeugkasten links auf der Heckplatte angebracht. **A2** Die belgische Armee war der erste ausländische Kunde für den neuen Kampfpanzer, und der erste Leopard 1BE wurde 1968 geliefert. Abgesehen von kleinen Änderungen - so waren z.B. ab 1975 seitliche Staukästen an der Wanne angebracht und die Kanone wurde mit einer Wärmeschutzhülle versehen - hat sich das äußere Erscheinungsbild des Fahrzeugs bis Mitte der 90er Jahre kaum verändert. Auf dem Inset sieht man die belgische Flagge, die für den CAT 89-Wettbewerb angebracht wurde, sowie die regulären Kennzeichen, die auf dem Fahrzeugbug und auf der Heckplatte angebracht waren.

B Dieses Fahrzeug ist mit einem Kanonenabschuß-Darstellungsgerät an der Bordkanone versehen und trägt den auf der Kanonenblende angebrachten Schießscheinwerfer. Obwohl es sich hier um ein mit den neuen Funkgeräten SEM 80/90 nachgerüstetes und als Leopard 1 A1A3 bezeichnetes Fahrzeug handelt, trägt es noch den gelboliven (RAL 6014) Anstrich. Die Turmnummer "456" auf der Zusatzpanzerung am Turmkorb weist auf die 4. Kompanie hin, während es sich bei der schwarzen "984" auf gelbem, quadratischen Grund um eine nur für diese Übung geltende Kennzeichnung dieser Einheit handelt. Gezeigt wird das Kennzeichen dieses Fahrzeugs sowie das Bataillonswappen, das auf der Heckseite des Turmstaukorbes geführt wird. Links am Turmkorb wurde eine zusätzliche Kraftstoffkanisterhalterung angebracht, die nicht der Standardausstattung entsprach.

C1 Die mit einer von Blohm und Voss entwickelten Zusatzpanzerung am Turm nachgerüsteten und mit der EMES 12 A3 ASFL-2 Feuerleitanlage ausgestatteten niederländischen Fahrzeuge werden als Leopard 1V (Verbeterd, d.h. verbessert) bezeichnet. Die gelblich grünen Kreuze kennzeichnen dieses Fahrzeug als Teil der "Agressorstreitmacht aus Grünland" während der Übung "Free Lion", die im September 1988 vom I. (NL) Korps durchgeführt wurde. Auf dem Inset sieht man zwei Beispiele für die breite Munitionspalette, die von der 105 mm L7A3 Kanone verschossen werden kann (in diesem Fall von belgischen Leoparden): Links ein M393A2 HEP-T (High Explosive Practice-Tracer, d.h. Sprenggeschoß, Übung, mit Leuchtspur) amerikanischen Ursprungs, und rechts ein L50A2BG TP-T/DS (Target Practice-Tracer/Discarding Sabot, d.h. unterkalibriges Übungswuchtgeschoß mit Leuchtspur) britischer Herkunft. **C2** Dieses Fahrzeug zeigt den von der Bundeswehr entwickelten Fleckentarnanstrich (FTA), der sich aus Bronzegrün (RAL 6031), Lederbraun (RAL 8027) und Teerschwarz (RAL 9021) zusammensetzt. Später wurden diese Farben auch von anderen NATO-Staaten übernommen, einschließlich den USA, wobei letztere die Farben als Grün (FS 34094), Braun (FS 30051) und Schwarz (FS 37030) bezeichnen.

D Dieser Leopard 1 (Fahrgestell-Nr. 6019) stand lange Zeit als Umlaufreserve in einem Depot, bis er im Dezember 1989 in Ischendorf überholt und auf den Rüststand A1A2 gebracht wurde. Anschließend diente er bei der Erprobungsstelle 71 in Köln, bevor er schließlich ins Motor-Technica-Museum in Bad Oeynhausen kam, wo er heute ausgestellt ist.

E Das Fahrzeug ist ganz in Gelboliv (RAL 6014) gehalten und trägt keine zusätzliche Tarnung, was bei einem Manöver recht ungewöhnlich ist. Dieser Leopard 1 A3 war Teil der BLUEFOR, wie das blaue Zeichen am Turm mit der schwarzen Zahl "901" deutlich macht. Nur sehr wenige Leopard 1 A3 erhielten den Fleckentarnanstrich (FTA), bevor sie aus dem Dienst genommen und verkauft wurden.

F1 Die 4th Canadian Mech. Bde. Group war Teil der Kanadischen Streitkräfte in Deutschland (CFE). Ab 1989 erhielten die ersten Fahrzeuge im Zuge der normalen Überholung den NATO-Tarnanstrich. Der gezeigte Leopard C1 ist das Fahrzeug des Führers der A-Schwadron, gekennzeichnet durch die schwarze "1" an den Seiten und auf dem Werkzeugkasten am Heck. Als weitere Kennzeichnung wird hier die "22" gezeigt, sie wurde am Fahrzeug des Zugführers des II. Zuges der B-Schwadron geführt. Abgebildet ist auch das taktische Zeichen des Panzerregiments der 4th CMBG. **F2** Im Herbst 1993 bestand die DANSQN, als Teil der UNPROFOR, u.a. aus zehn Leopard 1 A5DK (drei mit Räumschaufeln und drei mit TWMP), einem Bergepanzer 2 (von den Niederlanden angekauft) und vier M 113 Schützenpanzern. Abgesehen von den üblichen UN-Kennzeichen trägt dieses Fahrzeug eine dänische Flagge auf der rechten Seite der Blende und auf dem Werkzeugkasten am Heck. Die schwarze "47" auf gelbem Kreis ist das MLC-Schild.

G Der FlaPz 1 Gepard A1 - auch als B2L bekannt - ist mit einem Laser-Entfernungsmesser auf dem Radom des Zielfolgeradars an der Turmoberseite ausgerüstet, welches hier ausgeschwenkt und einsatzbereit gezeigt wird. Die weitere Abbildung zeigt das taktische Zeichen der 3. Batterie des Flugabwehrregiments 2, das auf der Luftansaughutze auf der vorderen Bugplatte und auf der Heckplatte geführt wurde: Die Zahlen links vom taktischen Zeichen benennen die Kompanie bzw. Batterie, die Zahlen rechts davon nennen das Regiment (bzw. das Bataillon).